A PREACHER'S LEGACY

A PREACHER'S LEGACY

David Pawson

Anchor Recordings

Copyright © 2017 David Pawson

The right of David Pawson to be identified as author of this Work has been asserted by him in accordance with the Copyright, Designs and Patents Act 1988.

First published in Great Britain in 2017 by
Anchor Recordings Ltd
DPTT, Synegis House, 21 Crockhamwell Road,
Woodley, Reading RG5 3LE

No part of this publication may be reproduced or transmitted in any form or by any means, electronic or mechanical, including photocopy, recording or any information storage and retrieval system, without prior permission in writing from the publisher.

For more of David Pawson's teaching,
including DVDs and CDs, go to
www.davidpawson.com

FOR FREE DOWNLOADS
www.davidpawson.org

For further information, email
info@davidpawsonministry.org

ISBN 978-1-911173-27-4

Printed by Lightning Source

CONTENTS

1. Ways of Preaching   9
2. Discovering the Structure of a Passage   27
3. Preparing, Starting and Finishing   43
4. From Content to Method   65
5. Conviction   83

This book is based on a series of talks. Originating as it does from the spoken word, its style will be found by many readers to be somewhat different from my usual written style. It is hoped that this will not detract from the substance of the biblical teaching found here.

As always, I ask the reader to compare everything I say or write with what is written in the Bible and, if at any point a conflict is found, always to rely upon the clear teaching of scripture.

David Pawson

1

Ways of Preaching

My first sermon was a failure. I was around nine years old and there was a congregation of three: my mother, my elder sister and younger sister. My father was away with the car one Sunday and we couldn't go to church so my mother said, "We'll have a service at home and you, David, will be the preacher." We turned an armchair backwards and I knelt in that and used it as a pulpit. I chose for my first sermon the parable of the labourers in the vineyard. I read the story first, then I told it again in my own words, then I went through it a third time drawing lessons from it, and finally my elder sister, in a tone of exasperation, said, "Isn't that vineyard full yet?" The whole thing collapsed into unseemly mirth and was a complete failure. I didn't try preaching again for another ten years.

When I was seventeen my parents' faith became mine and I began to preach then. At first I didn't preach in churches, I preached in the open air—in working men's clubs, down a coalmine, in pubs, anywhere there were people. I began preaching outside churches. My preaching at that stage is what I call "testimony preaching", and that was my beginning. I was sharing experience and that's all. My first sermon in church came one Sunday when I went to have tea with a converted bookmaker in County Durham called Jack Harrison — an amazing man. He gathered about 120 young people and he discipled them. I went to have tea with him and then we got on the bus to go to a place called Spennymoor in County Durham. On the way there I asked, "What are you preaching on tonight, Jack?" and he said, "I'm not preaching tonight, you are" — and he pushed me into the pulpit. I gave my testimony, I quoted every text I could remember, and I gave them all my theology in seven minutes flat—a feat which I have never been able to reproduce.

So that is how I began preaching in churches, which is far more frightening than preaching in pubs or working men's clubs. When you face a typical congregation, it is really weird.

I came from a line of preachers and three books remind me of this. One of them, *The Letters of John Pawson*, was written by one of John Wesley's first helpers, his very close colleague, and it contains his letters to Wesley written in 1794. The second book is *Harvesting for God* – by my grandfather, David Ledger Pawson. He died when I was four, so I don't remember hearing him preach. In fact I can hardly remember him at all, but he was an evangelist to his fingertips and he worked mainly in the North and the Northeast.

The author of the third book, *Hand to the Plough*, was my father, who was a professor of agriculture in Newcastle University. He did his evangelism on the weekends. Every Saturday night he interviewed people and made himself available. His great gift was friendship. It was through friendship that he led people to the Lord, and he kept a book in which he wrote the name and address of everyone he had led to faith, and there are twelve thousand names in that book (which I still have). He did that in his spare time, and he was a lay-preacher with a Methodist Church. All this is telling you that my background is Methodist—or it was. When I was called into the ministry, it was the only ministry that I knew, so I became a Methodist minister.

Then I began the second phase of my preaching, which

was what I call "text preaching": "My text this morning is John 3:16..." – that is how most Methodist preachers preached and so I just adopted the same thing. It is a highly subjective approach to preaching because you are selecting the text, and you either select a text that appeals to you or a text on which you can hang your own thoughts. It is really not very good preaching but I adopted it, and I marvel that I wasn't stoned to death for some of the early sermons! I still have the notes.

One I preached from the Authorized Version, which I never use now, but I did in the beginning. I thought this a marvellous text from 2 Peter, speaking to the churches then. Peter said, "You are a peculiar people...." I thought, "What a marvellous text and what a wonderful truth in that text! When you look around the pews we are a very peculiar people." I didn't know then that that was an old Elizabethan English word for belonging exclusively to someone. So I launched into it; "You are a peculiar people, just look at you..." and I made a great deal of that word "peculiar" in quite the wrong sense. I am amazed at the patience of congregations!

So my first phase had been *testimony preaching*, sharing my experience, and my second had been *text preaching*, in which I took a verse. But since there are only 34,000 verses in the Bible I could only deal with one thirty-four thousandth of the Word of God in each sermon. The selection was entirely up to me. Nobody every taught me to preach. I have never really thought about that until recently when I was asked to speak about it. I learned intuitively to preach, and I learned most from the faces in congregations. I learned from the response of people to what I was saying. I learned to stop talking when they stopped listening.

Then phase three in my preaching was what I call *topical preaching*. Now I would use a lot of texts in one sermon, gathering them from all over the place—all out of context.

I was then preaching *concordance sermons*. You choose a topic like "humility", you look up every text on that, you throw them together, and then you've got a sermon with a lot of texts. I then bought a big book which I confess I have never used: *Nave's Topical Bible*. In it, every verse in the Bible has been reproduced under topical headings. At first I thought, "What a help this could be to my preaching," but then I thought, "But why didn't God do this? Why did he give the Bible in the way he did? Couldn't he have given us books of the Bible on each subject? Wouldn't it have been wonderful if Genesis was all about heaven and Exodus was all about hell and Numbers was all about judgment, and something else?" But God didn't do that. I began to ask, "Why didn't God give us a topical Bible? It would have been so much easier to look things up and to preach if everything was in the same place." So Nave's is a book that I don't recommend. That big, heavy book is a waste of money.

But I got into *topical preaching* and instead of choosing a text I began to choose a topic. Whatever the topic, look up all the texts, put them together and you've got a sermon! I am disturbed that most preaching that I hear today is topical preaching—it sounds biblical because many texts are quoted, but when you look at it closely it is not very biblical. So I moved on.

By this time I found myself in the Royal Air Force as a chaplain. I found that fascinating. There were three chaplains on every station: Roman Catholic, Church of England, and OD—other Denominations; "oddballs"! I was the "odd" chaplain and when a bunch of new men arrived at the station, the Church of England demanded first pick and he said, "Everybody come with me," and three-quarters left. Then usually an Irish chaplain in a broad Irish brogue invited all Roman Catholics to follow him, and about another ten percent would leave—and I was left with the rest: Methodists, Baptists, Presbyterians, Salvation Army, Buddhists, Hindus, atheists, agnostics, and I really enjoyed being a chaplain to atheists. When I met an atheist I said, "Now I'm your chaplain, if anything happens to you I've got to bury you. I promise you that I won't mention God, I won't pray, I won't read from the Bible, I'll just say, 'This man is dead and gone', and that's all I'll do." I discovered that many are happy to live as atheists but they are not so happy to die as atheists—that's a bit risky. I was posted to Aden, in Arabia, where my first encounter with another religion, Islam, began.

Before joining the RAF I had been used to preaching in "lifeboat churches". Do you know what I mean by that? — women and children first! But now I was confronted with hundreds of men and my old sermons went down like a lead balloon. Text sermons didn't do much for them, and topic sermons didn't do much for them either. So I decided on a radical change, and I announced that I would take them right through the Bible from Genesis to Revelation in a few months.

I began that perilous task, and we raced through the Bible from beginning to end. This made such an impact and it was a complete change in my preaching. I became a Bible teacher. I would define preaching as "telling the whole truth to the whole man", and I began to do that. The result was amazing—the men began to get a big vision; they began to see God's purpose and began to feel, "This is something big enough for me to get my teeth into." It was really those few months that changed the whole direction of my preaching. It became my ambition to preach the whole Bible to whole people. By "whole people" I mean to their minds, to their hearts, and to their wills, and we will deal with that in more detail later.

That was a turning point in my life. Not only for the Bible, but as it happened for my relationships with Islam. If you had told me then I would, years later, write a book warning Britain about Islam, I would have thought you were crazy. But if you have read my book *The Challenge of Islam to Christians*, you will know that the Lord has led me to predict that this country will have Islam as the dominant religion, and we need to be aware of that.

I came out of the RAF reluctantly because something had happened to my theology in relation to baptism. Where I was posted, every Muslim who was baptized was murdered. They were knifed, their houses were burnt down with their families inside, and I thought, "What is it about Baptism that does this?" They didn't mind if they were coming to church or reading a Bible, or even saying they were a Christian, but the day they got baptized they were killed.

I thought a baptism was dropping a few drops of water on a baby's face, then I realized that the Muslims have a more biblical view of baptism than I did. They saw it as a burial of the past – the final goodbye to the old life. I began to think again, and the result was that I was coming back into civilian life where I was expected to "do" babies. We had one child by then; two came later, but I never got them 'done'. The Chairman of the Methodist district of South Wales wanted me to come to Tonypandy, to the Central Hall there where one famous member became Speaker of the House of Commons (Lord Tonypandy). ("Chairman" was the Methodist equivalent of Bishop.) I told him, "Well, I'm sorry but I can't do any babies any more." He looked at me and said, "Well, David, I'll give you a deaconess to do all the christenings if you'll come." I thought, "That's dishonest," and said, "No, I can't expect someone else to do what I'm not willing to do myself."

So they hauled me before the Methodist Conference Doctrinal Committee—which sounds impressive, and it was.

I faced half-a-dozen Methodist theologians to answer for my heresy. One of them had written a book in which he had said that only the Baptists are true to scripture, and I quoted him. He was there sitting facing me to judge me. So what they did was to pack me off to an unknown little place in Lancashire and we rejoiced in the address: 21 Eliza Street, Ramsbottom, Lancashire. You can't get more Lancashire than that! I didn't do any babies; I just couldn't go on like that.

There was also another crisis building up. I was learning to preach the Bible now— the whole Bible—and it was not very welcome. There were other preachers in the circuit (as it was called) who were much more liberal than that, and indeed I was followed around by a leading preacher who had a sermon entitled, "New Lamps for Old: The Magic of Fundamentalism." He was preaching that human nature can't be changed and you can't be born again. You see, in the Methodist Church, a group of churches come together in a circuit and you travel round the circuit, and so you only need two or three sermons every three months. You can then take them around, but being followed around by someone who was denying everything I taught became an unbearable, unequal yoke, and I resigned from the Methodist church. I remember saying to my wife, "We're going to lose my job, home, pension, everything."

I will never forget what she then said, "I want to be married to a man who obeys God" – and that was it. So we lost everything, and we lost nothing.

Within a very short time I was pastor of a Baptist church. I had to appear before the Baptist Union to be approved and they said, "Now as a Methodist minister, you've only had to produce two or three sermons a Quarter, do you think you are capable of producing two a Sunday?" I almost laughed; I had been longing for the opportunity to do just that. So I moved to Chalfont St. Peter in Buckinghamshire.

For the first time I had the opportunity of staying with the same people and taking them through the whole Bible. My target at that stage was to go through the whole Bible in ten years. Roughly, that meant a chapter every service, but that was the aim and the object – that if someone could put up with me for ten years they would have been with me in every part of the Bible, every chapter and every verse. So I began a totally different kind of teaching: taking a chunk of the Bible, a whole chapter, and sometimes with the Old Testament books two or three chapters each service, and taking people through them. Little did I guess what that was going to lead to.

There was a man in the congregation, Chris Ramsey, who was the first person in the church to get a tape-recorder— one of the old Grundig recorders with big spools. He said, "Would you mind if I recorded your sermons to take to the elderly and the sick?" I said, "Fine; that's a lovely idea." So he began to take them around, but when people began to hear the tapes they began to lend them to other people – and to others, and to others! Quite quickly I found myself with a rather larger congregation than I had ever had.

The first time I heard my taped voice preaching was a horrible experience! Do you remember the first time you heard your voice? You think, "Oh, I don't talk like that; I haven't got an accent like that." It is an eye-opener. When you see yourself on DVD, that is even worse. "Where did I develop that habit of pulling my ear?" You suddenly realize what an extraordinary person you are.

Anyway, it spread and spread and I became known as an evangelical Bible teacher— invited to conferences and congresses and other things. Then I had to go and ruin it all! I became a Charismatic, and suddenly all my Evangelical friends were cool. That is putting it mildly. So now I was in a different ball game and it all happened the week before

Pentecost Sunday. I had been preaching a series of sermons on the Holy Spirit leading up to that, but that Sunday a young man came up to me and said, "What's happened to you this week?"

"Why do you ask?"

He continued, "Well, this week you know what you're talking about," which was a very blunt comment but it was the truth. I had got all my knowledge of the Holy Spirit out of books and lectures but now I knew what I was talking about. It shut down a lot of doors of ministry, which was rather sad. Most of them have opened up again, but for some years some of them were tight shut.

So that was my style of preaching, and that has been my major style through my ministry. Three more phases were to follow, but that main style of expounding God's Word systematically and consecutively is such a joy. What I would later miss most in a travelling ministry was the opportunity to *build up* people's interest in a book of the Bible, so that people would come hungry, expectant, excited to learn more.

So that went on both at Chalfont St. Peter and then in Guildford, and I am going to describe how I prepared those studies. One of the key things was preparing an analytical outline of the passage. I always gave my hearers the outline, first on a big blackboard and then on a handout, a service paper. I wanted them to follow me and see the shape and structure of the chapter or passage we were looking at. I have found that structural analysis to be perhaps the most important part of my preparation, and I have fallen into the habit of alliteration in the outline. Do you know what that means? It is rhyming words by their beginnings or endings. We will look at that later. What a help it can be, and what a hindrance it can be too!

All that lasted until about 1989, and I had reached a crisis. I was already beginning to travel the world following the tapes. I was already being invited to do more work outside the church than inside, and I came to the point where I realized you cannot do both. You just can't both be a pastor of a local church and have your people wondering where you are this week. So I went away to a pastor's conference and said, "Lord, this week please tell me which you want me to do: to travel or to stay in one place." One of the conference speakers, Alex Buchanan, had a real prophetic gift. At the end of his talk he said, "I have four words for four men in here." He said, "I don't know who they are, but you will know." Well, the first three words I can't remember, but the fourth went straight into my heart: "My son, you have ministered to the extent of your gift in the place where I've certainly put you. You are no longer bound to stay in that place. I set you free and I set the land before you, but one thing I require of you—that you surrender all that remains to be done in that place into my hands, for it is my church and my congregation, and I want you to go out and sow. Serve me, that one day you will look into my face and say, 'Lord, we did it.'" That is all that I want to say—to look into his face and say, "Lord, we did it."

In the decades after that I have been a tramp for the Lord, running around the world like a headless chicken, but it has totally changed my preaching. It had to because I no longer had the opportunity to preach my way through a book of the Bible. I no longer had a consecutive pulpit. I am only in a place for two or three days at the most. What do you preach then? Well, I found myself into a new phase which I call *burden preaching*. As I travelled around and saw different churches, I developed burdens —and the burden became the preach. There were things in the churches that shouldn't be; there were things not in the churches that should be. I found myself focusing in on these things that were missing, or the things that were present and shouldn't have been there. When

I developed a burden I began to preach it, using the Bible that I had come to know, to highlight that point and to challenge that situation. So I found myself travelling around church after church, sharing the burden, particularly with ministers and pastors. I developed a real heart for my fellow pastors, and I realized that you are not going to change a church until you change its leaders.

So I gave priority to church leaders: pastors, elders, clergy and so on—and shared the burden. But after a bit I thought: this is the most inefficient way of sharing a burden. I could spend the rest of my life in a jumbo jet going from place to place sharing one single burden! I said, "Lord, there must be a better way to share a burden than this." I remember opening my Bible to Jeremiah and I prayed, "Lord, please show me how could I do this more efficiently." I've even got the date against a verse (18th April 1985): "This is what the Lord the God of Israel says: write in a book all the words I've spoken to you." I had never written a book. I had no ambition to write a book. I didn't want the hard work. I loved preaching, but writing—that is hard work. In preaching you see people in front of you; writing a book you are on your own, and you are just writing. I battled it down with the Lord. I said, "Lord, alright I'll begin to write books."

One of the first burdens I got as I travelled around was the number of Christians who have not been properly birthed. When you asked them how they were born again, and listened carefully, there was something missing that should have been there. From my study of scripture I came to the conclusion that there were four things necessary for a healthy baby to be born properly. They were: repent toward God; believe in the Lord Jesus; be baptized in water, and receive the Holy Spirit. I discovered that there were Christians of years who had never got all four. They were firing on three cylinders, or two, or even just one — they had believed.

Some had never been baptized; some had never received the Holy Spirit, and I learned from my New Testament that believing in Jesus and receiving the Holy Spirit are two quite different things. Some of them had never repented properly.

When Christians came to me with a problem I would say, "Well tell me how you were born again. Tell me how you began." I listened carefully and when I realized there was something totally missing there I said, "Well let's get that put right first and see what happens to your problem." Invariably, the problem either disappeared or became small enough for them to deal with. The way we start the Christian life affects the whole Christian life unless we have a second "bite of the cherry" and make up what has been missing.

Well, I began to speak about this burden—about how to be born again properly, how to begin the Christian life as a healthy baby. I began to write the first book called *The Normal Christian Birth*, which like every British publication has to be classified by the British Library. They classified that book under "Gynaecology" and it went into every public library in the medical section! It is not the only book I have written that was misunderstood. Another book seriously misunderstood was the one on hell that I wrote (*The Road to Hell*), because as I have travelled around I ask congregations, "When did you last hear your preacher talk about hell?" and I had discovered it had hardly been preached. So this became a burden. I shared it verbally first, and then, when I felt I had understood it well enough, in a book. So this was a new style of preaching altogether—*burden preaching*. It was, I believe, more prophetic than pastoral. Pastoral teaching, I believe, is teaching people the whole Bible systematically so that they really understand it. So I would still call myself a teacher, but I would say I am a prophetic rather than a pastoral teacher now, when I am sharing a burden.

The Lord still had a surprise for me: a few church pastors

in Wallingford (in the Thames Valley), got in touch with me. They said, "David, our people are not reading the Bible for themselves. Can you do anything about it?" I said, "I'll try; I'll come once a month to you and we will look at one book in the Bible in depth. My aim will be: first, to get them so interested in that book they can hardly wait to read it; and second, to give them enough background information so that when they do read it they understand it. I'll come for four evenings, once a month." I continued, "I'll come on these conditions: first that you all read that book of the Bible before I talk to you; second, that you all read it again after I've talked to you; third, that all the house groups will study that book; fourth, that all the preachers will preach from it for the next month." At the end of four evenings the pastors came to me and said, "David, can we please book you for the next six years?" I said, "I might be in heaven by then," but I did it, and once a month I went to Wallingford and took them through one more book in the Bible until we had covered the whole Bible. This was a new phase for me; it is what I call *book preaching*. It is bigger than chapter preaching—it is taking a whole book in the Bible in one study.

We tape-recorded those talks, which went everywhere. So somebody finally said to me, "David, you'll have to do this on video." I replied, "Oh no, not another six years!" But we did it! Recordings were made which became DVDs, and *Unlocking the Bible* as I called it became a whole series. When we finished the videos I thought: What a relief! All done. Then the publisher Harper Collins said, "David, we want all this in a book." I responded, "Oh no! Not another six years!" But we managed to do it by taking the soundtrack from the videos, transcribing it and editing it. A young man helped me to do this, and then I edited the final version. The result was a book that is going around the world, and no one is more astonished than I am. It has sold more than 150,000 copies so far in English. It has been (or is being) translated into Spanish, Portuguese, Finnish, Italian, German, Indonesian, Chinese and Korean, and the work continues.... The most encouraging thing is the letters that have come saying, "I'm enjoying my Bible again." That is what the whole thing was about. So do get it if you haven't got it, or give yours away and get another. So this was *book preaching*, and it was a big surprise.

There is one category of preaching that I haven't mentioned, which I call *gospel preaching*. I am no good at that; I have tried, but I can't do it. First, because my gospel is too complicated and I don't think there is such a thing as "the simple gospel". Some people can do it. Last week I was sitting at the feet of Reinhard Bonnke, who says that he has led fifty-five million Africans to the Lord through his evangelism. That is an amazing claim, and I listened to him preaching. The way he handled the Word of God makes my hair stand on end, but evangelists get away with it. Have you noticed that? They really do. They can make the Bible say anything they want. Part of his sermon was the difference in the flames on the heads of people at Pentecost. He said some had a little flame, some had a big flame, some had a blue flame, some had an orange flame. He went on, saying, "God has a flame just to fit you, and the size and colour of the flame will be just your size." I thought, "Help! Where does he get that from?" A lot of it came from his imagination, but there was no doubt about it that healing was his big gift. People came because they saw healing, and he matched his preaching with action. "Word plus deed" is pretty powerful, but "word plus sign" – there it was. I have to say, "Well, Lord I'm not an evangelist." I am so glad I am not, in a sense, I am too fond of the Bible. But I did have one year as an evangelist, living in a caravan. The most profitable part of that year was meeting my wife, but there were some who came to the Lord. You know, it is great when you find out what you are and what you are not, and you don't try to be what you are not. I am a teacher and that is what God has gifted me with, and I use it for his glory. It doesn't mean that nobody gets saved under the ministry. I have found that when you teach God's Word, that converts people, it reaches people, and funnily enough he can use the most unlikely part of his Word to touch someone.

I was preaching my way through Ecclesiastes, and we had more people converted through that than any other series. When you read Ecclesiastes you think, "Help" – but I remembered we got to chapter five which says, "Be careful about your words, because God recalls everything you say." That is a frightening thought. Sitting in the congregation one night was Charles Colson, who was connected with the tapes of President Nixon, and altering those tapes to cut out words that were on it. After the sermon I invited him to share his testimony with us, and he got up and said, "You've already heard it. Ecclesiastes 5 was my life, and it was the record of all our words in the White House that finished me off." So Ecclesiastes spoke to that man, and I have found that teaching the Word of God has as much evangelistic fruit as anything, though of course, it is not directly aiming at that.

But I have never tried to preach gospel sermons. I can't put it on in twenty to thirty minutes, taking people through all that they need.

In summary, what did I discover through these various stages in my preaching? I began with experience or *testimony* teaching, when everything was my experience. Of course, if you are limited to your experience you will never talk about heaven or hell because you have not experienced them. I moved from that to *text* preaching; giving a verse and then expounding the verse—highly subjective selection, ignoring the context. Then I moved on to *topical* preaching, which is probably the favourite style of preaching today in many fellowships. Then I moved on to *passage* preaching—a whole chapter or even more, but preaching a whole chunk, and that was when I found my ministry. Incidentally, that was when God opened the wider door to my ministry. He put a seal on that phase, which he had never done until then. From then on he opened the way, and I said "for his glory" and it opened up 120 countries to my preaching. It included all six continents, including Antarctica, and scientists at the South Pole continued watching me. So I discovered then that when you preach the whole Word of God systematically, consecutively, God will open doors for that. He wants that. He wants his whole Word – what I call *contextual* preaching – and we will go into that in much detail in the next section: putting the Word of God into its context, not just its context in the Bible, but its context in life. When God spoke, he always spoke in a life situation. God never gave sermons. He spoke to particular people in a particular place, at a particular time, in a particular situation. When you put the Word of God into its context like that, you understand it so much better. So that was my basic way of preaching, and that is the one that God took worldwide, but then having lost my pulpit I had to revert to *topical* preaching, or what I call *burden* preaching. Then I got to *book* preaching, and that really was the climax of my ministry. God has opened a wider door for the book preaching than he ever did before.

I had my biggest ever congregation, which I couldn't count, in the largest church in Taipei (Taiwan), which seats 1,500 to 2,000, and the pastor had forbidden his congregation to come. He had arranged for an overflow in another large auditorium elsewhere in the city and he said, "Now all my people go there, so visitors can come here." So that meant two full, large auditoriums in Taipei. Then I was told we were sending some form of link-up to forty other churches all over

Taiwan. So those packed churches were listening too. Then he said, "We are broadcasting it on television to the whole of China." So there I was, stuck in the Church of Living Bread in the middle of Taipei, preaching to I don't know how many, and I thought, "Well, this servant of God began with three and now the Lord is giving so many listening people." Praise him! I never planned that; I never expected it, but there it is. So at eighty I was still going strong – but not very strong with my throat I am afraid, yet nevertheless I was still going, and willing to keep going as long as the Lord gives me health and strength.

Those were the phases, so that in a sense my preaching has had to change five or six times, depending on the context. You must apply all that we look at later in this study to *your* context and to the openings God has given *you*. He will honour his Word, and if we don't have his Word I've got nothing to say. I am not interested in peddling my opinions. They are not worth anything, but I will go to the ends of the earth to tell people the truth of God's Word, because it is the truth that sets people free. Having said all that, there is more to it than that, as you must realize.

2

Discovering the Structure of a Passage

Let us now begin to imagine that you are with me in the study. How do I prepare my messages? I have to tell you that the one thing you will desperately need if you are going to be a preacher is time, and time on your own. I used to reckon it took me an hour on my own in the study for five minutes in the pulpit, and I am not a brief preacher, but that is the kind of time I reckon I needed. I gave it priority over anything else because I regarded it as the most important thing I could do for my people—to feed them with the truth. So come with me into the study and I will try and re-create a time of preparation.

The first part I would call meditation: just thinking—sitting and thinking. Sometimes I sit and think and sometimes I just sit, but just sitting isn't very fruitful. By my side I have my Bible. Look at your Bible, examine the edge of the pages and you will find whether you are reading the whole Bible or just favourite bits. My Bible was falling to pieces when I was in Romania. The pages were literally falling out and a young man came up to me one morning and said, "Would you give me your Bible please?" I said, "What for?" "I want to do something with it," he replied, and off he went with my Bible. He brought it back re-bound, all put together, and even transparent sticky tape on the pages that were torn, and so I got my Bible back. I said, "You couldn't have given me anything better than my own Bible back." Bibles are like shoes or old slippers. You get so used to the old ones that new ones are horrible. I hate to change my Bible, and I thought "the time has come". Literally, the pages were dropping out when I read it to people in Romania, and the young man saw that – and he was a bookbinder.

In the study you have a Bible, you also have a stack of clean white paper and a pen. For the first part of preparation you must not have anything else. What you do is this: you have got a passage to read and you read it, and you read it, and you read it, and you read it. Even reading it aloud is helpful because you will get more meaning out of it when you read it aloud – if you have got the right meaning, which you may not have.

There was a man in Yorkshire reading, and he read the words, "We speak that we do know." You realize what he was reading: "We speak, that we do know" – very different. The very way you read the word "Emmanuel, God with us" tells you how you understand it. You can say, "*God* with us," or, "God *with* us", or, "God with *us*".

Reading it aloud, you will find yourself getting different meanings out of it. At the same time as you are reading, reading, reading, write down every thought that comes to you, whatever it is. It may be crazy, it may be off centre, just keep writing down everything that comes to your mind as you read that passage—everything. You will finish up with half-a-dozen pages of the most scrappy notes you can imagine, but that is the beginning. Don't, whatever you do, read someone else's sermon at this stage because the temptation is to pinch it if it is any good. I had three tons of books at home but there is not a single volume of somebody else's sermons in my library. Though I enjoy listening to other people, I never tempt myself to pinch their sermon. It is your own—you want to give *your* sermon. God wants you to be you, not imitating someone else. There are certain ways of speaking. Even the word "God" – I can tell you what preacher someone has been listening to by the way they say "God". If you are copying someone else, don't. God wants each of us to find our own way of doing it. Nevertheless, I am just telling you how I do it and you can ask the Lord whether you should try the same.

So that is how I begin. I want it to be my sermon and nobody else's. I want to get the truth for myself, because if I get it for myself I can get excited about it, and if I can move myself I am going to move other people. My wife will tell you that very often when I am preparing, I get up off my seat and walk up and down, wearing the carpet out, and I am almost beginning to preach to myself. If you get excited about a passage of the Bible you can know that your people will get excited as well. If you are not excited, don't expect them to be. So begin with just paper, a pencil and your Bible, and start writing down every single thing that comes to you.

It is like cooking a meal – cooking it takes far longer than eating. Preparing a good meal takes time, and though it may be consumed in twenty minutes, it may have taken a couple of hours to get ready. You are feeding people with the Word of God, so time is very important. There is no shortcut. Meditating on God's Word is the first step.

One thing you can do at this stage is to look at different translations of the Bible. My basic one is the New International Version, but I have a volume of the New Testament from twenty-six translations (and they have started doing the Old Testament too). I find that very helpful. Read all the different translations and see if that brings other thoughts to your mind. A cross-reference Bible is helpful at this stage — that has text references down a centre column or at the side, to look up related passages. That can be useful too. Let me say a word about this: chapter and verse numbers were not God's idea, and they are not inspired by the Holy Spirit. The chapter divisions were the work of Steven

Langton, a thirteenth century Archbishop of Canterbury. Then along came a printer from Paris who had a long journey from Paris to Lyon by carriage, and to while away the time he divided the chapters into verses.

Now both those developments have an advantage and a disadvantage. The advantage, of course, is that it is much easier to look up the scripture. People often criticise me for not mentioning chapter and verse numbers, but I follow the apostles. They only mentioned the book. They said, "It's in Isaiah," and the people who heard the apostles had to go and search the scriptures. Nowadays people just go and look them up. It has made it convenient for cross-references and so on. The disadvantage is much bigger than the advantage. You can get the Bible now without chapter and verse numbers. My friend in America LaGard Smith, a legal Professor, has produced the New International Version without chapter and verse numbers. People who have got it tell me the Bible becomes a different book. They read it like they read any other book now. Instead of reading just little bits, they read whole sections and they read whole books through. That has made a big difference to their Bible reading. So you can get it without chapter and verse numbers, but for preparing they are useful. Personally, my rule is rarely if ever do I quote chapter and verse. I will quote books. For example, did you know that God whistles? That is in Isaiah. You may ask where – well, you read Isaiah. You won't have to read too far actually, but twice he says that God whistles. I am so glad, because I whistle too.

That is phase one. I am rushing through the preparation because after I have got all my thoughts down on paper, still I am not going to look at other people's yet. I will do so later, but my second stage is the most important for me and that is to *analyse* the passage, to try and understand its structure—the shape of it. I have spent lots of time analysing scripture for its structure. Once I have got that structure I have got the skeleton of my teaching. I then have to put flesh and clothes on it, but I need to get this skeleton first.

Consider what I might do with Psalm 23. My first way of structuring a passage is to do it in the language of the passage, or my own language, but I don't try to do more than that. So I do my first analysis of the passage. There is verse one, then verses two to six. Verses two to six are a description, but verse one is the key to the whole Psalm, for it is who he is. "The Lord is my shepherd; I shall not want." Of course the word "want" there is better translated now by "lack", but that is the statement. Where the scripture says "the LORD" we know that in Hebrew that is the Lord's name: "Yahweh". "Yahweh is my shepherd." It is saying the God of Israel is my shepherd. That particular God is the One who looks after me; so verse one stands on its own.

I call that "who he is", and it raises the question "who is *your* shepherd? Who are you expecting to look after *you*?" It is saying there are many gods around, many different names, but it is saying: "There is one God who is my shepherd, and it is *the God who has revealed himself in Israel*." Verses two to six are obviously *how he cares for me*. We notice again a change of the pronouns. In verses two to three, the pronoun is "he"; in verses four to five "you"; and in verse six "me". There is a change of focus there through the verses. Again, if you know the Psalm you have probably noticed all this. I have got my two main subjects: *who he is* and *how he cares*. Then I divide the second half into three sections under "he", "you" and "me". What does he do? I have written down, "There are four things that the psalmist says he will do: he makes me lie down in green pastures; he leads me by still waters; he restores my soul (or, literally, my life), and he leads me in paths of righteousness for his name's sake. Each of those phrases is so meaningful.

In the Middle East there are no green fields. There are patches of green grass in the desert and the shepherd must know where they are. He will lead his sheep to the green pasture, and, when the sun is at the height of its power in the midday, he literally takes a piece of string and he ties the four legs of the sheep together and pushes them over. I have got photographs of that happening. He makes me lie down, and that is a very powerful expression. The psalmist is saying: that is how I feel sometimes— he has pushed me flat on my back, he has made me lie down in green pastures.

Then, "He leads me by still waters." Did you know that a sheep's nostrils are next-door to its mouth? Therefore it can't drink rough water, or the water goes up its nostrils and it drowns. So a sheep has to have *still* water, and he, the shepherd, will know where the still water is that the sheep can drink. He will lead them by still water.

He restores my life when I am exhausted. Sheep very quickly get tired, especially when you have to go miles to find food or drink, and you can't just be turned into a field. The good shepherd knows when the sheep need to be restored, rested, and: "He leads me in the right paths for his name's sake." The whole point of that section is for *his* name's sake—for his reputation. The shepherd is doing it not so much for us; it is for himself and his reputation as a good shepherd, because every sheep bears the name of the shepherd, and sheep reflect how well they have been looked after. You go to a sheep market and watch the farmers looking at the sheep they are going to buy, and they know who has been a good shepherd. It is for the shepherd's name's sake.

Then in verses four to five it is much more personal, to "you", and he is talking about what this shepherd does for him—that he is without fear in the valley of deep shadow. This is not the valley of death. I know this psalm is a favourite at funerals but it has nothing to do with death. It is going through a valley where there are shadows, where there are caves, where there are hollows in the rock where wild animals crouch and wait for the sheep to come. This sheep says, "I am not afraid of evil because you are with me. You have given me courage", his rod and his staff comfort. The rod is a sort of cudgel—a short piece of wood with a big knob at the end and the shepherd will use that, not on the sheep but on the wild animal. He will also have a crook, which he puts around the neck of the sheep and pulls it away from the wild animal. David is speaking about his experience as a shepherd here when he had to use the cudgel—the rod on the bear and the lion that were crouching in the shadows. We go through the valley of shadows all through life. It is not the end of life here. That comes later, but in the middle of life we are going through a valley where we are under threat, where there are evil forces waiting to attack. With the shepherd we don't fear that. He is big enough to deal with them.

"He prepares a table for me in the presence of my enemies" – the lovely picture there is of a man sitting down to a big meal and all his foes are around him. It is a humorous picture as he is tucking into his good meal and he doesn't care about all his enemies around.

"You anoint my head with oil." Sheep's heads are very vulnerable. There is no wool on them and they often have wounds on their heads from all kinds of things that they rub into or run up against. I have seen shepherds soothing wounds on sheep's heads.

Actually I have been a shepherd. My first job on the farm was sewing open lambs' eyelids. Many lambs are born with dropped eyelids and therefore they are going to be blind, and you take a needle and thread and sew the eyelid to the eyebrow, sewing it open. After a bit, the muscles of the eyelids will take over and the thread will rot and drop out. That was my first task as a shepherd with these poor little lambs, trying to sew their eyes open with a needle and thread. Caring for sheep teaches you an awful lot about the Lord. Then, finally, he looks to the future—his future—*me*. I like to talk about the shepherd's two sheepdogs: goodness and mercy. The two sheepdogs will follow me all the days of my life. Finally: Dwell in the House of the Lord forever. It is a lovely psalm.

Well now, what have we done? We have looked to the structure of it and the structure has given us two main headings, and then three small headings, and then, further, under the first "he", four little headings. I call this the, "A1, a(i) Method"—capital A, big 1; lower case "a", little (i). I use that to find the structure of a passage. Once you have opened that up you have got the bones on which you are going to build your sermon. I have already started building it, but then I like to put it into a more easily remembered form. We have got the structure, but one of the ways to make it more memorable is alliteration. Now I know all the things against and for this, but I have found it helpful to me. It is a much easier structure to remember when it rhymes. So I tend then to take the structure that I have written at the top of my paper and put it into alliterative form.

I changed the main headings to: "The shepherd looked to" and, "The sheep looked after", because those are the two themes of the psalm. Under "The sheep looked after", I have: "The Provision the shepherd makes for them; the Protection he offers them; and, the Prospect for the future he offers". So that has neatly turned the structure into an alliterative one. I take it even further into smaller headings: "Provision"; Restful Pastures; Refreshing Pools; Restoring Periods, and Right Paths. Under "Protection" (that he gives us): Courage, Comfort, Confidence, and Consecration. Under "Prospect": Right through life and Long after death. I have even managed to take those two a little further and label them "Goodness and mercy", and "In his house forever".

There we now have an outline. That is all it is, but it is a much more easily remembered outline than the first one. It is easier for me to remember and easier for people to remember as well. Alliteration has been called the province of fools, poets, and Plymouth brethren. I am not a Plymouth brother and I hope I am not a fool, but I am a wee-bit of a poet, and I like poetry. The New International Version shows you the poetry by the layout of its print. The prose looks like a newspaper column and the poetic passages have gaps between each line. Much of the Bible is poetry, and that is for a number of reasons, but you tend to remember poetry much better than prose. "The boy stood on the burning deck, whence all but he had fled." Do you remember that? So easily we remember poetry, and therefore poetic headings help.

Now there are two things needed here. One is a rhyming dictionary. Did you know there was such a thing? It tells you all the words that rhyme in their beginning and all words that rhyme at the end. You just look at one word and you have got all the rest. That is a great help to get an outline like this. The other help is a thesaurus that gives you words that mean the same thing. The easiest I have found is The Reader's Digest Family Word Finder, but you can get a thesaurus very easily. You look up the word you want to match and it gives you several words that mean the same thing, and you can choose one that fits; I'm afraid I do that.

The classic case of alliteration is a sermon on the Prodigal Son. The three main headings are: his madness, his sadness, and his gladness. Under "his madness": he cavilled, he travelled, he reviled. Under "his sadness": he went to the dogs, he ate with the hogs, and he lost his togs. Under "his gladness": he got the Seal, he danced the reel, and he ate the veal. That is a terrible outline, but I have remembered it so easily – it just fits. The disadvantage is when you are stuck for the last word and you really try and force a word in to fit. God must be a poet because he speaks in poetry so often. Many of the prophecies are in poetry. It is so that people can remember it easily, so I am not ashamed to use alliteration for my outlines.

Let us move on to a passage that is more complicated – an outline of 1 Corinthians 13. What I am trying to impress on you is that time spent on analysing the structure of a passage pays off enormously. I would always spend a lot of time on this phase, really seeing the structure, how it builds up. It tells you things about the passage you may never have thought about. You know the passage very well. I developed an outline before I preached the chapter. There are clearly three parts to the chapter, which in most Bibles have been divided into three paragraphs. The first three verses are clearly about the necessity of love—that without love you can do nothing, you can be nothing. "Nothing" is a strong word, but without love it is all wasted. So one to three I give the title, "The necessity of love". Four to seven talk about "the quality of love". Notice that I am using the end of the words to rhyme—necessity; quality.

Verses eight to thirteen are clearly about "The superiority of love"—that it is greater than everything else. So we have got our main headings, now let us analyse each of the sections into further detail using our "A1, a(i)" method. Verses one to three divide into two clear parts. Verses one to two are about the gifts that God gives us. Verse three is about the gifts we give to others. In verses one to two the theme is, "If I have gifts from God but haven't love, I am nothing"; verse three is, "If I give, I gain nothing" so there is a clear parallel here between gifts that I have received from God and gifts that I give to other people. In the first case I *am* nothing; in the second case I *gain* nothing.

Let us look at the gifts in more detail. He mentioned three—gift of tongues, gift of prophecy, gift of faith. These are all spiritual charismata given by the Holy Spirit to us, but even if I have all three and lack love, then I am nothing, just a big noise. Tongues: they can be tongues of men or of angels, but even if I speak them all and lack love, I am nothing. Prophecy: I may fathom all mysteries of knowledge and be able to prophesy and tell people everything they want to know, but I am nothing. Faith to move mountains—I've not got so much faith. Jesus said, "If you have faith as big as a mustard seed you can tell a mountain to jump in the sea, and it'll go." I know some people in Japan who did.

There was an orphanage in Japan, which was six storeys high, and bounded on three sides by a public street, and it was run by the Japan Evangelistic Band: JEB. They were full of orphans which they had either found on the streets or been given, and they had too many orphans in the house. The missionaries discussed this situation. They said, "Well, we can't build any further up because we are in an earthquake zone and six storeys is the maximum. We can't build out on the street that side, or this side, or the front." At the back was a very steep hill right up against the building, and one of the missionaries joked and said, "Of course, if we had faith we'd tell the mountain at the back of the orphanage to jump in the sea." The other missionaries laughed at the joke, but one or two of the children heard that and took it seriously. They went to the Lord and said, "Lord, please will you throw that mountain in the sea, so that we can have more orphans in the orphanage?" They went away on their annual holiday and when they came back the hill had gone, and it was level ground. The missionaries were astonished, but the children weren't. They just said, "But we asked Jesus to throw it in the sea." The missionaries were not content with that answer and they made inquiries as to what had happened while they had been away. Apparently it was a large seaport town and the council had decided to fill in the sea to make more ground, to build more warehouses for the ships, and they had wondered where they could get enough dirt to throw in the water. The council had suggested, "What about that hill behind the orphanage?" So for a week while they had been away, earth-moving plants moved in and took that soil and threw the whole thing in the sea to make more ground for the ships.

I have a photograph of the building at home — it challenged my faith. Children sometimes have a much stronger faith than adults. We are too sophisticated; we have objections; we have questions. Even if you had faith to tell a mountain to jump in the sea and you don't have love with it, you are nothing. That is a very strong statement—nothing. Not even a little. You are nothing. What about what I give to other people? Well, I could give all my possessions to feed the poor, and in the world's eyes that would be great, but without love in it I would gain nothing. They would gain a lot, but I would gain nothing. I could even become a martyr and give my life to be burned at the stake, and still if I am lacking love I gain nothing. Well that is the *necessity* of love. It is absolutely necessary if you are going to be anything or gain anything.

Now the middle section of the chapter is the one that is read at weddings. I don't know why, because the love you are celebrating at a wedding has nothing to do with this. You are celebrating *eros* or (best term) *philio*, but this is *agape* here. Now every marriage needs agape, but very few have it. So that is a good reason to read it. I usually read the Song of Solomon at a wedding. That is much more appropriate, but Paul is not thinking of weddings at all here. He is thinking of normal church life. I know you could recite the middle section, but when you analyse it a strange thing emerges.

DISCOVERING THE STRUCTURE OF A PASSAGE

First of all, it is a sandwich. Paul begins on a positive note, and tells us what love is. He then moves on to a negative note and tells us what it isn't, and what it doesn't. Then he goes back to the positive again, as to what it does. There are two sides to love: what it is and what it does. Both are necessary, and we need to understand what agape is and what it does to get the picture. To get the clearest picture you need to know what it isn't, and what it doesn't. You see, a preacher has to define things in two ways: positively and negatively. We are to teach the truth and we are to teach what is error. We are to teach what is right and what is wrong. Sometimes you can define anything negatively much more clearly than positively, and there is more negative here then positive. Start with the positive, and we notice that the positive sections are concerned with other people. The negative sections are concerned with yourself. Love is right when it is thinking of others and wrong when it is thinking of itself. So the negative and the positive make up this full picture.

We begin with what it is towards others. It is patient and kind. Lovely words: patient, kind. Then we move on to the negative. What it doesn't, and here we are concerned with self now. It doesn't envy other people and it doesn't boast. It neither feels, "Why don't I have that?" nor does it feel, "I have that and you don't." Again there is a very clear definition here of what it doesn't do. Then we come to the central one: what it is not. Love is not proud, it is not rude, it is not self-seeking, it is not easily angered. Now defining it negatively like that challenges the reader of it to say, "Where do I fit in all this? Does this describe me or someone else?"

Then he moves back again to what it doesn't, and you notice that even in the negative section there is a sandwich between "doesn't," "isn't," and "doesn't." It is a very careful structure here. Once you have seen the structure of a passage, you understand how the writer of it is thinking. It is a very orderly chapter. Then he goes back to what it doesn't. It doesn't keep a record of wrongs done to it, and it doesn't delight in evil. Then he goes back to the positive again – what it does do: it rejoices with the truth, it always protects others, it always trusts, it always hopes for the best, and it always perseveres, even when it is disappointed.

Now do you realise that in the positive side, all the way through, he is describing Jesus? Every positive thing he says about love you could say about Jesus himself. In the negative things he is talking about us, and we are really challenged. Is there any trace of this negative in me?

So much for the middle section, but you see again we have found the skeleton of the passage. We found the shape of it: this positive, negative, positive. Then the more detailed "what it is at the beginning" and "what it does at the end" and, in between, "what it doesn't, what it isn't, and what it doesn't". These are very careful, systematic descriptions of love. Had you seen all that in this chapter before? You have now seen a shape to this passage which will colour your thinking from now on, and make it much easier for you to teach it to other people because you will remember the structure and that will be the skeleton of your teaching.

The final part of the chapter is clearly about the superiority of love. Therefore it is, first of all, contrasted with temporary things. Paul goes back to prophecy, tongues and knowledge. He says all these things will pass away; they are only here for a time. They are like the scaffolding on a building, which is removed when the building is finished, and once the church is built, this can come down. So the key words there are "pass away". Then he uses a different approach by highlighting the change between "now" and "then". "Now we see through a glass darkly, but then face-to-face." Actually, the word is "Now we see in a mirror darkly", and in those days they didn't have silver mirrors like ours today. They had polished copper mirrors, and you could see through them darkly. You couldn't get a clear image with them. But then we shall not need a mirror, we shall see face-to-face.

We only see God now in a mirror. We see him in the faces of saints, we see his creation reflected in the beauty of the trees, but it is all a reflection and not a clear view. You can look at nature; you can look at human nature and see a reflection of God's image, but that is all you can see. One day you will see God face-to-face. Now; then. Now you are like a little child; one day you will mature and you will put away childish toys. Of course a boy did that in those days at a specific age when he literally threw away his toys and became a man. I wish we had such a ceremony in our society when a boy becomes a man. Some men are still boys, and the only difference is the price of their toys.

You see the Jews have the Bar Mitzvah, and when a Jewish boy reaches that age he puts away all his childish things and he becomes a man. Paul says that is how it is going to be with us. We will put away the toys. He is saying charismatic gifts are toys—of course they are tools as well to build up, but they will all go. I was once preaching to two hundred doctors and I said to them, "In heaven you will all be out of a job." One doctor shouted back, "And so will you, David!" He put me in my place thoroughly, but yes, we'll have different jobs up there. Put away childish things.

Now he reaches the great verse. He says, "Now faith, hope, and love last." They are permanent. Prophecy, tongues, and knowledge are temporary; but faith, hope and love – permanent. They will survive all the time, and, even among them, love is greater than faith and hope, because love is the nature of God. We never say, "God is faith" or, "God is hope." We do say "God is love", and that is the greatest thing of all: to be restored to the image of God – and that means to be love. So again you see that working on the structure of a passage has really revealed more to us of what it is all about, and where it is going and how it was made up. I don't know if Paul thought his way to this, or whether it just came naturally to him, but there is an order in almost every passage of scripture, which opens it up to you.

3

Preparing, Starting and Finishing

What I often do in this stage of my preparation is to translate the Bible passage into my language. It becomes what we call a paraphrase. It is not a word for word translation, but I sit down and try to put the passage I am going to preach into my language. I am going to do this with the letter of Jude. It is a small letter but we shall find it will open up in new ways to us. It is the second last book in the New Testament, greatly neglected, and even more greatly needed in our day. Here is my translation of it.

This letter is from Judas, who I prefer to be called Jude — one of the bought slaves of King Jesus and a brother of James, whom you all know. I am addressing all those over there who have heard and responded to the call of God our Father and enjoy the love of his family and so far have been kept safe by your relationship with his Son, Jesus. May you experience more and more of his undeserved mercy, inward peace, and loving care. My dear friends, I had fully intended to write an encouraging note about the wonderful salvation that you and I share, but I now find I must send you a solemn warning and appeal to you to fight on for the old faith which was first given to the believers once and for all.

I have heard that certain men, who shall remain nameless, have sneaked into your fellowship. They are not in touch with God. Their sentence of doom was pronounced and recorded ages ago. They distort the amazing grace of our gospel into an excuse for blatant immorality and indecent behaviour. They deny that the Messiah Jesus is the only true Head and Lord of all. Now I want to remind you of some facts you are already familiar with, which warn us not to trifle with God. Remember that he brought a whole nation out of slavery in Egypt yet destroyed most of them because they would not go on trusting him. Nor are his angels any more exempt than his people. When some of them deserted their proper place and function he took them into custody and is keeping them in the lowest and darkest dungeon until their trial on the great day of judgment. Likewise, Sodom and Gomorrah gluttonised themselves with debauchery, hankering after forbidden pleasures, just as the angels had done. Their fate in the fire that burned for so long is a sober omen for us all.

In spite of such examples from the past, these interlopers abuse their own bodies, despise the authority of the Lord, and deride the angels in glory. In contrast, when the archangel Michael argued with the devil about the disposal of Moses' body he did not presume to condemn him or slander directly but simply said, "The Lord is the one to reproach you." But these men among you don't hesitate to malign what they don't understand and what they do understand is based on natural instinct rather than supernatural inspiration, as if they were animals without reason. Woe betide them, they walk in the same way Cain went. They plunge into Balaam's blunder for the same profit motive, sharing the rebellious attitude of Korah—they will come to the same ruin. They think they are shepherds but they are not interested in feeding the sheep, only themselves. They are like clouds driven away by the wind before they drop any rain, like uprooted trees in the autumn with neither leaves nor fruit—dead as dead.

Like crashing wild waves of the sea casting up the foam of their shameful behaviour, like shooting stars, destined to disappear down a black hole forever—it was about such as these that Enoch, in only the seventh generation from Adam, made a prophetic announcement, "Look out! The Lord is coming with hordes of angels to carry out his sentence on all the godless people for their godless deeds which they have done, and all the godless words they have spoken against God himself and his godly people." These infiltrators are discontented grumblers, always complaining, pursuing their own ambitions, full of big talk. They even use flattery to gain their ends. But you, my dear friends, need to remember the sombre predictions of the apostles themselves—they said that as history enters its final stages there will be those who are contemptuous of godliness while they pursue and practise the very opposite. The result will be splits among you initiated by those who follow their fleshly impulses, strangers to the Holy Spirit.

As for you, my dear friends, reinforce yourselves while becoming more mature in your faith, praying regularly in the way the Spirit leads you. Stay within the boundaries God lovingly set for you as you patiently wait for the return of our Lord Jesus Christ and the everlasting life he will bring in new bodies. Deal gently with those who are wavering between you and the interlopers. Do anything you can to rescue those who have already gone over to them, as you would snatch a child from a burning house. You must even feel compassion for the villains themselves, but alongside that, keep a healthy fear of being contaminated by them, even by their stained clothing. Now let's praise the one who is able to keep you from slipping into all this and enable you to stand before his glorious throne, blameless and jubilant. To the only God who can save us and bring us to glory belong radiance, majesty, all power and dominion, before all time all through history and for evermore.

I have divided the letter into three parts: the past, the present, and the future. These are the three dimensions in which we have to live. All of us have a past, a present and a future. The major part of the letter is learning from the past and this is where the warnings come in. The point of reading the Old Testament is to learn from it. What happened to the people then is relevant to our condition today. He is emphasising the history of the people of Israel and he is writing to a Christian church and he is saying, "Learn from their history." Too many people today are not studying the Old Testament. In fact, there are some teaching that the Old Testament is such an unchristian book that we shouldn't read it. They are saying the God of the Old Testament is different from the God of the New. That heresy was started by a man called Marcion centuries ago. It is a very common idea, not just outside the Church but inside also—that the Old Testament God is somehow cruel, harsh, that he believes in ethnic cleansing. That has been said by a leading evangelical today. But, in fact, the reason for reading the Old Testament is: (1) Divine nature has not changed, God is still the same; and (2) Human nature has not changed. Therefore, everything in the Old Testament can tell us something about God and something about ourselves. If you do not learn from the past you are condemned to relive it. You will have to learn it the hard way yourself. The easy way is to learn of how God dealt with them and will deal with you. So the first part of the letter is an appeal to the past and how God dealt with people who corrupted his people in the past.

In verses twenty to twenty-three he moves on to

themselves, first of all telling them how to conduct themselves in the present, in light of the past; second, how to conduct themselves towards others, and mentioned three particular groups; then the final two verses, which we all know and love, that God is able to keep us from falling and present us faultless before his throne. He is the able God and the only God and our future is secure in him. I think you have probably realised by now that once I have got to the structure of a passage, everything is downhill after that. It is uphill until I have really mastered a passage. So let us look at this in greater detail. It has got the usual introduction: the sender, the address, and a greeting. That is all straightforward, but then there is an unusual feature right at the beginning. He says, "I wanted to write to you about our shared salvation, but I am having to write to you about fighting for our faith." The reason is that there has been infiltration of the fellowship by bad teachers and he says their condemnation was written long ago. So that is a sort of introduction.

Then we find out what has gone wrong: first of all, their corruption is a corruption of *creed* – what they believe, and of *conduct*—how they behave. Here was the word I had to struggle to get: the cogitation, the way they think, their character, their conversation and what was their motivation—what compelled them to do what they were doing. So we have six bad things about these infiltrators.

Then he says, "Their condemnation was written long ago." He makes five appeals to the past: to the history of Israel, history of Moses, history of Enoch, and so on. He says the five things that they will face in the future: their retribution, their punishment—in other words they will lose respect, they will cause rebellion, their revelation is questioned; and, above all, their ridicule. We shall see each of these things.

Now when I got as far as that, I suddenly realised that he cleverly interweaved their corruption and their condemnation. With each thing that is wrong, he gives the corresponding result of that from the history, so that he is systematically detailing their corruption and then their condemnation—corruption, condemnation. I note with each of these the things that have been corrupted and the things that the writer is saying will happen to them from olden times.

There are two things that they are corrupting in creed. First, they are corrupting the doctrine of grace and making it a licence for immorality. That is what was happening in South Africa that I was asked to speak about when I went there, all centred on the word "grace". The other thing was that they were denying that Christ is the Lord of all. They were putting him alongside other people. These are the two corruptions of our beliefs that are still happening today. Once you take those two wrong turns in your creed everything else goes wrong.

In their conduct they were polluting their own bodies, they were rejecting authority, and they were slandering angels. That is quite a package. In their thinking, the things they don't understand they abuse, and the things they do understand are things that animals could understand. Once again, a pretty strong condemnation. Their character is described from nature in four ways—they are like fleeting clouds, fruitless trees, foaming waves, and falling stars. Those are lovely illustrations of the kind of character they have, and of course, they produce drought, death, debris, and darkness. Their conversation is a clear mark of such people. They are grumblers and fault finders, they follow their own desires, they boast about themselves, and they flatter for advantage. Now all this is a very detailed description.

Then they use compulsion. The last one: they are divisive; they divide a fellowship very quickly between those who follow them and those who don't. They follow natural instincts rather than spiritual guidance and they simply don't have the Spirit. Now, what a list of things about these people who are wrecking the fellowship, but they would and that is why we have such a strong letter from Jude. You can wreck a fellowship in one generation, and especially young fellowships, when somebody comes in and takes them over and leads them the wrong way. But all this helps us to recognise someone who will be dangerous in the fellowship.

With the condemnation side, notice how he goes straight from one to another all the way through. He talks in terms of the Exodus generation—all but two of them never made the Promised Land—that is a very striking fact. Then he mentions fallen angels. I believe that is a reference to Noah and the story of what was happening before Noah's flood. You had there an extraordinary sexual liaison between angels and humans. The Bible is very clear that we are to have sex with our own level of life and no other. Therefore the Bible is very strong against animals and people having sexual intercourse and between humans and angels. The initiative here was the angels', and the result of that illegal liaison is what the Hebrew says is "Nephilim," translated "giants" in Genesis 6. We don't know the translation actually—it means a hybrid creature. It was neither angel nor man, but it was a strange being that they had created but God hadn't.

Then Sodom and Gomorrah is the other example. Sodom and Gomorrah were still burning in Jesus' day; we know that from the historian Josephus. You could literally walk a mile or two from Jerusalem and see the smoke rising from the south end of the Dead Sea, where Sodom and Gomorrah had been destroyed by an earthquake but also by a release of oil from that area, burning pitch. Jesus, when He referred to Sodom and Gomorrah, was referring to something you could go and see in that day. The south end of the Dead Sea is drying up at the moment and everybody is waiting to see

Sodom and Gomorrah re-appear in our day. That would be an extraordinary revelation for our generation. The writer of Jude mentions the fact that the flames are still there.

Then he got on to the fact that these infiltrators didn't show respect. He appeals to the time of the archangel Michael and his battle with the devil for the body of Moses. Now, that is not in your Bible, but it is in the Apocrypha. It means that when Moses died and his body lay there, God sent an angel to bury him. Angels can cook, they can do lots of things that we can, and presumably they can wield a spade. An angel was sent to bury Moses and the devil said, "You can't have him, he's mine." From one point of view the devil was right. Moses was a murderer. He had killed an Egyptian. The devil argued with the archangel — "He's mine, you are not to touch his body." The archangel didn't argue with the devil, he respected him to the extent where he said, "The Lord rebuke you. The Lord deal with you. I'm not going to." There was a respect there for the devil and we need to respect the devil. He is a good deal cleverer than all of us and needs to be not joked about but treated seriously.

Their rebellion: Jude instances Cain, Balaam and Korah. You know what Cain did—he killed his brother. You know what Balaam did, when the king against Israel tried to get him to curse Israel and all he could do was bless him. Korah was one of the rebels against Moses who was swallowed up in an earthquake. All this is saying: in time, people who destroy a fellowship will pay for it and they need to be warned against the results of what they are doing. To destroy the church is to destroy the Body of Christ. That is a very serious thing to do and people who do that will pay for it.

Then he moves on to the revelation of Enoch's prophecy. Enoch was the first prophet of all. It is not mentioned in the Bible but it is in the book of Enoch. It was only the seventh generation after Adam and they needed a prophet. When I read that bit I noticed that the word "godless" came four times. Enoch warned against the godlessness of godless people that live a godless life. That is the biggest sin of all: to be godless. It means to ignore God, to live as if he doesn't exist. Frankly, it is the life of so many of our fellow countrymen at this moment—they are living godless lives. They may not be "bad" lives, they are just godless — no reference to God. They live as if he is not there, as if he doesn't exist. It is not just declared atheists like Richard Dawkins, it is ordinary people who just live godless lives, self-centred lives. Godlessness is a very serious thing for people made in the image of God to do. Their end will be what is described here.

It is interesting that Enoch was the first prophet because the one thing we are told about him is that he "walked with God". It is a lovely description of a godly life—a godly person is someone who walks with God; it is as simple as that. Enoch one day went for such a long walk that God said, "You might as well come to be with me, you are too far from home now." Enoch walked with God and he was not—a shock for the relatives but lovely for Enoch. Wouldn't it be lovely to go for a walk and finish up in glory? But that was Enoch, he was a prophet. God always warned people before he punished them. Every time. God is fair, he is just, and he will never punish anyone without giving them a warning first. He has his prophets who will tell people what faces them if they go on in the same way.

Well now, I have felt that as soon as I got the outline of Jude and the structure, that I was over the hill of preparation and that I could now begin to build around the outline. So I am just telling you how, in practice, in the study I prepare a passage to preach. To summarise: I prepare first by getting all the thoughts down that I can, and then I work very hard at the passage itself and get the shape of the bones of it. Once

I have got that I can preach it. Of course, preparation is not over yet, but the bulk of it is. I find when I have got as far as that I could get up in the pulpit and take people through Jude profitably, but there is more to it.

We now turn from analysis to putting flesh on the bones and putting the clothes on the flesh. Or, to put it differently, adding the meat and adding the gravy. Now some preachers are all meat and no gravy and some preachers are all gravy and no meat. But they need each other. We need to put strong meat to people but we need to put the gravy on to make it palatable and enjoyable. So we have got our skeleton. I need more paper now. I then spread the skeleton over as many sheets of paper as needed, each major heading and subheading on a separate sheet.

Then I have to ask: What do I need to say about each of these to help people to get the meaning? Whether it is a major point or a minor point, what do they need to know to understand it? So I begin to add to the bones the flesh: Well, I need to tell them this, I need to explain that, or I need to illustrate the other. So I build up on this skeleton we have found, this structure, and build around it. I have deliberately kept quotations from others to a minimum. I always feel that I would be showing off that I had read from other people, or that I was giving second-hand stuff. You may have noticed I very rarely quote anybody else. But there are some things worth quoting, especially if the person is well known to the hearers. My brother-in-law, a Methodist minister, used to say in the middle of a sermon, "As a famous preacher once said..." My sister, married to him, thought about this a bit and said, "You said that, didn't you, last sermon?" and he said, "I know." So he was always quoting this famous preacher who was himself. I don't recommend that, but I liked his sense of humour.

So you are now building up the flesh on the structure,

on the bones. Now come the clothes. I am referring now to illustrations—stories. People love a story and, if you can, tell a story, especially if it is true. A little boy said to his father, a minister, "Daddy, was that story true or were you just preaching?" A deadly thing to say! Yes, it can be fiction as well as fact, but telling a story can always get interest. Perhaps that is why Jesus used stories so much, but the whole Bible is a story. It is in the framework of narrative and that is a good example to copy.

Now let me tackle this question of: Where do you get your illustrations from? Some people I know are very systematic and amazingly careful with this. They hear a story or they read something in a book and then they file it in a filing index, under a subject such as "humility" or under a text. The late Dr. W. E. Sangster was a master at this. He had filing cabinets with thousands of sermon illustrations, all classified. He even offered me on one occasion, "David, if ever you want to use my illustration, please feel free to come and help yourself." I never did I'm afraid – though at one time I used to meet him about once a month. Nevertheless, I admired his skill in doing this, but he had also enlisted his wife and his secretary to do it for him. His wife would read a biography and write in the margin of the book "pride" or "humility" or whatever, and then the secretary would file them in the filing cabinet. When he prepared a sermon he would just pull the drawer out and: "Ah, here is the illustration." I have never been able to do that. I have tried on more than one occasion and the remnants of it are in my study, unused. I am not that systematic.

I confess to you freely that my method is Pelmanism – word association. As I am preparing a sermon, an illustration comes into my mind by association and it goes into the sermon. I don't recommend that, but I am just being frank with you. Jokes: one of the funniest jokes, which I have used when I was speaking in Jerusalem on Galatians, is all about circumcision. The joke I heard was that there was a man looking for a faith to live by – a Gentile man, and he studied all the religions of the world and then he decided that Judaism would suit him better than any of the others. So he found a local rabbi and he said to him, "I want to convert to Judaism." The rabbi had a long discussion with him and finally said, "Well, everything seems to be straightforward and you can convert to Judaism." "But," he said, "There is a small surgical operation involved. Did you realise that?" He explained circumcision to this Gentile man who asked, "Is it very painful?" The rabbi replied, "Well, I don't remember; to tell you the truth, I was only eight days old when it was done to me. Mind you, I do remember that I couldn't walk for a whole year afterwards." So I used that in Jerusalem to get people interested in circumcision, because it is not a subject of any great interest to your average congregation.

Jokes have a place and there is an awful lot of humour in the Bible. People don't realise that there is one verse in the Old Testament which, when I hear someone read it in church, I can't help giggling at: "And lo, in the morning, behold it was Leah." Now, if you know the story I think that is one of the funniest verses in the Bible. Here is Jacob waking up on the first morning of his honeymoon and he has got the ugly sister instead of dear Rachel. If that happened to you, you wouldn't laugh—but if it happened to your best friend you might. It is hilarious. Having pointed out the humour in that verse, you might then add, "But do you realise that this was the man that cheated everybody else?" – now chickens have come home to roost and someone is getting at him after he had got at his old blind father. Be sure your sins will find you out, or whatsoever a man sows, that shall he also reap.

You see how the humour has given you an open doorway to the truth. I will be coming back to this, but it is so important when you preach to help people to *feel* the Word of God. Most preachers are trying to persuade people to *think* the Word of God, and that is good—we have got to understand it. But to feel it is different, and you feel it when you can laugh, or when you can cry, or when you feel guilty. It seems to me that until we get people to feel the Word of God they won't be motivated to do something about it, just thinking it is too abstract.

So what can we say to make this point interesting, to make the food appetising, to put the gravy on the meat? Well, quoting anything contemporary from the media, especially television or (up to a certain age) quoting what happens in your family. There was a time when our three children came to me and said, "Daddy, if you mention us again in the pulpit we will blow the gaff about you." You can date my sermons from then on—no more family illustrations from that point. But family life is a source of interest and a source of real application and truth, so why not?

Biographies – and not just biographies of well-known Christians. There are too many illustrations that hold before people spiritual giants. You know, "... who sacrificed everything to rush off to Africa and be killed." Your people sitting before you just say, "That's not me. I can't identify with that – not yet, anyway." The more ordinary your illustration, the more ordinary the person is, the better. Then people are far more likely to say, "Well, that's me." In fact, I was preaching in Millmead one Sunday. There was a milkman there and suddenly in the middle of my sermon he jumped to his feet and he said, "That's just what happened to me!" Then he looked around and realised he was in church and wondered what he had done. But at least he was wrapped up in it; he was feeling it and he couldn't help it. I was thrilled with that response, though I think he was embarrassing himself.

You can have a filing system of illustrations but I call mine the "patent piling system". There are piles of cuttings and newspapers in my study. I think I know where they are, I think I can put my hand on them—until my wife spring cleans, then I lose them all! But whether your system is piling, filing or whatever, illustrations help enormously to convey the truth. People listen to illustrations, but they must illustrate. I was listening to one preacher and he told a very moving story and then he said, "I don't know what that illustrates, but it sure is a great illustration." I thought, "Well, he's honest", but they have got to illustrate as well.

Now the next bit of padding or filling out the skeleton is the introduction and conclusion. These are very important parts of preaching. The old saying is, "If you don't strike oil in two minutes, stop boring." That is not a bad little tag. My advice is: get to your subject as quickly as possible, preferably in the first minute, so that people know what you are on about, so they know where you are going. If you just spend five minutes even going around the subject, people will very quickly stop listening. So go straight for the jugular in your introduction, whether it is a story, a quotation or a simple statement.

One of the best openings I ever heard from a preacher was one of our professors in Cambridge. He was given the rare privilege of preaching the University sermon, which was on a Sunday afternoon at Great Saint Mary's with all the academic staff present. He got up and started like this:"I suppose the priesthood of all believers means that the Pope is sometimes right." He did this with such a straight face and immediately everybody was listening, immediately he got their attention. That I suppose is what a good introduction ought to do, to get the attention. I have found that often a question is the best introduction. I have jotted some of those down that I have used: Where was God in the Holocaust? What sins has Jesus saved you from? Why did God allow the tsunami? Now all of these have gone straight for the subject and they have done so in a way that gets people thinking immediately, because a question prompts an answer, and you are right into your subject. So that is my basic approach to an introduction. What will get their attention? What will get them straight into the subject? What will get them with me from the beginning? So much for the introduction.

Then I go to the conclusion and say to myself, "How am I going to end?" Reinhard Bonnke said, "It's the privilege of an evangelist to finish off his sermon three times." Paul, when he wrote to the Philippians, says "finally" three times. I am afraid that most preachers are guilty of not ending. However, my wife and I listen regularly to a preacher who stops when he has finished. He just stops and that is great. However, I want to say more than that. Somebody said to me early on in my preaching life, "David, don't finish without telling them what you hope they will do about it." I have never forgotten that though I have not always lived up to it. That is very practical preaching.

I remember one lady in Guildford who shook my hand at the end of the morning service and said, "Thank you for that sermon. I found it very moving." I'm afraid naughty me blurted out, "Where to?" She said, "What do you mean?" I said, "You found it very moving. Where did it move you to?" She turned around and stamped her feet and walked away. Just by the way she walked away I knew I had really upset her. So I resolved to try and patch it up at the evening service. When I saw her in the evening I said, "I'm terribly sorry I said that, but it just came out. I just couldn't help it." She replied, "Well thank you for saying it because all the way home the Lord said to me, 'Where to, where to, where to?' I finally had to be honest and I said, 'Nowhere Lord, I just found it very moving.' I've sorted it out with the Lord and he's moved me somewhere now."

I said, "I'm so glad for you." I was sorry I said what I did but in another way I was glad that I did say it. If you don't finish on a very practical level people are going to say, "Nice sermon, very moving," and go home the same as they came. What's the point? You are not in the entertainment business and neither am I. Keep it short—a conclusion that drags on is no conclusion. A conclusion should conclude.

Well now, I am still in the preparation stage, still in the study. I am going to talk in the next section about delivering what you have prepared in the context of a meeting or a service. Let me give you three little final hints. Number one: turn your material into notes. Don't ever take a manuscript into the pulpit or you will have eyes more on the paper than on the people. So even if you have written out a sermon, turn it back into notes before you preach. I heard of one vicar who got his latest secretary to take his sermon and produce it in note form on a series of postcards. In the pulpit he would just turn over one postcard after another and preach from her notes. But he never thanked her—never showed any gratitude for all the work she did. So one day he is in the pulpit and he turned over the next postcard and it said, "You're on your own now." I thought it was a very suitable response from a secretary who had been shown no gratitude. But we do need notes, though never a manuscript. You are so tempted to read a manuscript that your eyes are down most of the time and you look up now and again, and that is no way to preach. I will tell you now: I never wrote a single sermon out in my life. I have always preached from my notes and that meant that I was free to look at people.

Secondly, memorise the notes once you have got a structure as I have shown you. You can memorise that quite easily. I take full notes into the pulpit but I am pretty independent of them because I have memorised them. If you have a clear and alliterative headline method you can memorise that quite simply. It is alliterative, it is poetic, so it is easy to memorise. You have got that outline in your mind so you are not dependent on the notes even if you have them. If you have notes, then don't try to hide them. There was one preacher I know who used to say when he wanted to turn a page of his notes over: "And there, way on the hill called Calvary...." He tried his best to distract the listeners, but if you have got notes why try to hide them? If you have got a full manuscript, you are really tied to it—you almost have to read it.

So memorise it and then preach it to yourself or your wife. I am serious. I preach a whole sermon to myself before I preach it to anybody else. I am usually on my feet when I do that. Sometimes I go through to the kitchen and if it is acceptable I share what I have prepared with my wife. If she is a patient listener I preach the whole sermon to her and try it out. Your wife can be your best fan or your best critic.

One Thursday evening I got all the Sunday school teachers together and preached my Sunday morning sermon to them. That had a lot of advantages. One was that they got a sermon. Too many Sunday school teachers go out with the children and never get the sermon, never get fed themselves. It also gave me a dry run of the sermon. Between Thursday night and Sunday morning I could polish it up and realise what wasn't getting over and expand it a bit. Also, after I had done that on the Thursday, the Sunday school teachers got together in groups to prepare their lessons for the children. It really worked well even for the children because the teachers were co-ordinated and had thought things through first. But for me it gave me a rehearsal, if you like, and I was very grateful for that.

I have rushed you through preparation but I haven't finished with that. There were certain objectives that I had in preparation. The first was to make it all real; the second to make it relevant; the third to make it reliable. Let me explain those three things that were objectives for every sermon I preached.

First, make it real. We have a problem with culture. The Bible was written two thousand miles away and two thousand years ago. It is not in our culture. It is a rural culture most of it, not an urban culture. It is certainly not a technological culture — there is nothing about mobile phones or television in the Bible, it is a totally different world and you, as a preacher, are a guide in that world. You are showing people around somewhere, you are taking them to unfamiliar territory. You can bank on the fact that there is nobody listening to you who has been desperate to find out what happened to the Amorites. You may have prepared a sermon all about the Amorites, and it is a different world. Somehow you have got to become a guide to a world they have never lived in and don't know.

I love guiding people around Israel. Tourists are gullible— you can tell them anything and they will believe it and write it down. I remember telling one of the groups that the emperor Haile Selassie of Ethiopia claimed to be a direct descendant of the Ethiopian eunuch in Acts 8, and they were all writing that down! If you didn't laugh at that, ask someone to explain it to you. Nevertheless, it is great fun showing people somewhere they have never been. I have really enjoyed it. As a preacher that is what I am doing. I am taking people on a journey into a world that they have never lived in and a world that is so different from our world and somehow I have got to introduce it to them in such a way that they enjoy the visit. Now that is to make it real.

I have learned something from a television programme on archaeology. I wondered how the presenter got me interested in ruins of four thousand years ago. He did so because he was fascinated himself and also because he had the gift of communicating his excitement to others. This is our job as Bible teachers—we have got to be so fascinated ourselves with what we are saying that we are excited about it. That will come across in the way we talk. It is culture shock at the heart of this problem. The solution to it is to remember, as I have already told you, that human nature has not changed and God's nature has not changed. Somehow, bringing those two factors into a very different world, you are taking them back into the past. Take the stories of Abraham, Isaac and Jacob. It is lovely preaching those, but you are talking about people who lived thousands of years ago. Yet, given the way God dealt with those three men, you can really get people interested and involved.

I underline that it is important to emphasise the feelings involved. Too many people approach the Bible with a purely cerebral interest. But you can't deal with Abraham, Isaac, and Jacob without your feelings being involved. They were not good men—all three lied to save their own skin. When you get into the story you find out what it was that really made them our forefathers – that they believed God, they trusted and obeyed him. That was all. They were just ordinary people like us, with our failings and our weaknesses. Nevertheless, when God told them to do something they did it because they trusted him. That has made it human somehow. Jacob's cheating is all too real, all too human, in the world of today. We have a guide's duty to take them back into the past until they feel it and it is real to them. Then we have to bring them back into the present and make it relevant, and somehow relate the past to the present, and relate lives lived very differently to ours as we live them. How does what we have learned about then apply now?

Our second duty as guides is to bring them back into the present. There are dangers in doing that—the danger is that we translate things into our culture and adopt our culture. We have got to be very aware that our culture is not godly. You can, if you are not careful, bring today's thinking into this journey back into the present. To do this, some preachers spiritualise everything — they allegorise things, they don't apply it literally. I am thinking of the miracles of Jesus. People explain the miracles away to make it relevant and somehow find a scientific explanation for something that will make it relevant. That is adopting today's culture. We need to bring the point into today's culture. What would washing feet be in today's culture? Do you know why Jesus really washed the disciples' feet? Because they were dirty! It is as simple as that — they needed it. A modern day equivalent would be to wash each other's cars after we have arrived at church, wouldn't it? Because the cars are dirty and need it. Our feet aren't usually dirty in church. Jesus was not inaugurating a ceremony. He was meeting a humble need in a very humble way. The example to follow is not a foot washing, unless your feet are dirty and need it – because they did need it. Walking in open sandals on rocky, dusty roads, your feet get filthy. Especially because at meals in those days, they didn't sit on chairs, they laid down and reclined on the left elbow and so your feet were next to the next man's head. So, you don't wash your hands there, you wash your feet before you stick them at the nose of the next person at the table. What is the equivalent? Washing hands, or what have you. This is translating into our culture. But we have got to be careful that we are not destroying the Word of God in the process, and I could illustrate that.

For example, there is no doubt in my mind that scripture is patriarchal. I mean by this that the man is head of the family and the man is the elder of the church. We have got to ask ourselves the question: was that purely cultural or is that God's word to us? What are the male and female roles in church today? Should they correspond to the patriarchal society in the scripture or are we free from that now? I think you know my answer if you have read my book *Leadership is Male*.

It is not just a matter of making it relevant by coming back into our present, but by introducing a third dimension: our future. Whenever you apply the Bible you find yourself applying it to people's future, not just their present—not just their future in this world but their future beyond the grave. That is an essential dimension of biblical preaching. That is very relevant to people because everybody has a future and it is absolutely essential that they know what the future could be and what their choices in the present could affect—their whole future. That is part of the biblical message. So we take them back into the past, make it real. We come back into the present, and make it relevant. Then we go on into the future and make it even doubly relevant, because everybody has a future. I am afraid not so many people believe that today. I find that most people nowadays think that death is the end. Whatever they say, they live as if death is the end of everything – and that therefore there is no need to think of anything beyond.

Some years ago I was asked to preach to the Stock Exchange in London. They asked me for a title to advertise my visit. I said, "Well, tell them I will preach on 'You can't take it with you, and if you could it would burn.'" They flatly refused to advertise that title. So I said, "Alright, I'll cool it a bit. I'll speak on 'How to invest in the future beyond the grave.'" That is what they advertised and it is what I spoke on. But, you see, they were all buying pensions, they were saving up for retirement, preparing for this side of the grave, not beyond it. I told them how to invest your money so that you will benefit after you are dead. I said that a shroud has no pocket, you can't take anything with you, but you can invest in heaven. I told them how to from Luke chapter 16, where Jesus told you how to invest your money so that you will get a welcome in heaven. It is good to tell people, "Forget about your pension for a moment and think about investing a bit further ahead," but of course if you don't believe there is a further ahead you don't think about investing in it.

When I say make it real, make it relevant and make it reliable, what I mean by that is: *make it true to truth*. If we believe God's Word is truth, then we must preach what is true. How do I know if it is reliable? How do I know that it is truth that I am preaching and not just my idea of truth? Well, the answer is *context*. If there is one thing I want to affirm here that I hope you will not forget, I want to make a plea for *contextual* preaching – "contextual" meaning that if you want to be true to God's Word and have the right interpretation it is context, context, context that will keep you right. When you take a verse out of its context you are so liable to make it a pretext—your own idea. So context is the key every time.

4

From Content to Method

What I am pleading for is contextual preaching. Most people think that by context we mean the verses before a verse and the verses after a verse – the *immediate* context. Modern Bibles are helpful in dividing the prose into paragraphs and the immediate context is the paragraph in which a statement occurs. Without the paragraph you could get quite the wrong meaning of a verse.

Let me give you some examples. "I can do all things through Christ who strengthens me." Now I want you to think of something – any one thing – you can do with Christ that you couldn't do without him. Was money what you thought of? Well, that verse is about money, and its context is managing to live on whatever income you have. In the context, the paragraph, Paul says, "I have learned to be content with much or with little because I can do all things with Christ who strengthens me." I have discovered that two-thirds of some congregations are in debt and are rarely told that being in debt is stealing. You can steal in two ways: by taking something from someone else that doesn't belong to you or by withholding from them what belongs to them.

When you are in debt you are holding money from someone to whom it belongs. The Bible tells us not to be in debt. Through Christ you can get out of debt, and stay out of it. Now let me make it clear that having a mortgage on your house isn't debt, but getting behind on a payment is. In these times of pressure, people who have mortgaged themselves to the hilt are going to find themselves in debt and get behind with payments. So that verse becomes very relevant to preach today, but it is always preached in a very spiritual way that has nothing to do with money—but the context is money. The context is being content rather than covetous, and therefore, not buying things that you don't need.

Let us take another example: "In Christ," says Paul, "there is neither male nor female, Jew nor Greek, bond nor free, but we are all one in Christ Jesus." The feminists love that verse, the homosexuals love it, and they say, "In Christ there is neither male nor female" which, if it means that Christians are neutered when they are converted, means that same sex marriage is perfectly acceptable to Christians since there is neither male nor female. But the context of that verse tells us that it is about our vertical relationship with God, and not our horizontal relationship with each other. In the horizontal we are still male and female, and we still have different roles and responsibilities. In our vertical relationship with Christ, my wife is a son of God according to that passage because the context says that we have all been baptized into Christ, we are clothed with Christ, we belong to Christ, we have accepted his identity, therefore all of us, in God's eyes, are male, Jewish, and free because Jesus is male, Jewish, and free. We have all adopted his identity, and we are all one person in Christ Jesus. That is true vertically, it is not true horizontally. Once again, context changes the meaning.

Consider John 3:16. Do you know the most important word in John 3:16? It is a word of two letters: "so". What does it mean? It doesn't mean "so much" or "so deeply" as if we should read it, "God *sooooo* loved the world...." It doesn't mean that at all. It means, "Thus; in the same way; likewise." That is the word. "For likewise, for in the same way, God loved the world that he gave his only begotten

Son." In the same way as what? Well in the same way as the previous verse. People may know the verse but don't know the context, and you will not understand John 3:16 if you don't know John 3:14, 15 and 17. Those verses give the verse the meaning. "For likewise God loved the world." Like what? Like when he destroyed people with snakes for grumbling about the food he gave them. That is the previous verse.

Or take Matthew 22:14 (I have given you chapter and verse now, naughty me!). "Many are called, but few are chosen." The trouble is people reverse that and make the choice come before the call, but that is not it at all. The choice comes *after* the call. Many are called, but then few are chosen. It is the end of a parable that talks about a king's wedding feast for his son's wedding. He sent people out to invite them to come, and many of them turned down the invitation. So he said, "Go out and invite some more. Go out beyond the town into the country, persuade them to come in." He did that, and they all turned up for the king's son's wedding, but one man turned up in his working clothes. The king said to him, "Friend, why didn't you change your clothes for the wedding?" The man was speechless because he could have done, he hadn't bothered. So the meaning of the verse, "Many are called but few are chosen," means many will come in response to the gospel invitation, but those who don't bother to change will be rejected at the end. Do you hear the very solemn message? If you don't bother to change, you won't be chosen at the end for the Son's wedding.

Now all these verse I am giving you change their meaning with the context, which is the paragraph around the verse; the few verses ahead of it and the few verses afterwards, but that is not the end of context. The next context is the *section of the book* in which your text occurs. When you look at the whole section of a book, again meaning changes. Take one or two examples. 1 Corinthians 12–14 is a section in a book concerning spiritual gifts. Chapter 12 describes the gifts, chapter 13 describes the same gifts without love, and chapter 14 describes the same gifts exercised in love. So the whole section is not about love but about spiritual gifts.

Indeed, 12:4 begins: "Now concerning spiritual gifts..." and the whole section is about spiritual gifts. But we lick the jam out of the sandwich and we talk about the section on love, but it is a sandwich and it all belongs together. Psalm 23, which I looked at earlier, belongs to Psalms 22 and 24. When you put them all together you have the Lord presented to you as the Saviour in Psalm 22, as the Shepherd in Psalm 23, and as the Sovereign Lord coming to his own in Psalm 24. So, once again, people love Psalm 23 because it is nice and comforting, but you can't have the comfort of Psalm 23 without first coming to the Saviour of Psalm 22, which begins, "My God, my God, why have you forsaken me?" It goes on: "They have cast lots for my clothes," and, "They have pierced my hands and my feet." It is all about the Cross and until you have been to the Cross and found him as Saviour, you are not going to enjoy him as Shepherd, and you won't look forward to him coming as Sovereign. Who is this coming? It is the Lord coming; he is at the gates. So you see those three psalms help each other—they are the context for each other.

But that is not the end of context. Let us take one other example: chapters 9, 10 and 11 in Romans belong together; they are all about Israel. But Calvinists love chapter 9 by itself out of context, anti-Zionists love chapter 10 out of context, and crazy Zionists love chapter eleven out of context— but they belong together. Chapter 9 says Israel was selected by God in the past; chapter 10 says Israel is stubborn in the present; chapter 11 says Israel will be saved in the future. So the three chapters belong together. Whether you are a Calvinist, a Zionist or what have you, if you take one of those three chapters by itself you will come unstuck, you will get a distorted view. So context is not just the paragraph, it is the section.

Thirdly, context is the *book*. The Bible is not a book, I have got one version at home that is called "The Book" but it is not. It is a library of sixty-six books. The word "Bible" comes from the plural word "biblia", which means "books – plural". My books get misunderstood. When I wrote a book called *The Road to Hell* it was advertised in a national Christian magazine: "Read David Pawson's autobiography." People were buying it thinking I had called my life "The Road to Hell", but there we are! So *The Normal Christian Birth* was thought to be gynaecological, and this was thought to be my autobiography. Books can be misunderstood, but the Bible is a library of different kinds of books, and each biblical book is different from every other book. When you read anything in the Bible you read part of a book, and your first question of interpretation must be: Why was this book written? That is why I did the series called "Unlocking the Bible"— it is to look at each book of the Bible and ask: "Why was it written?" Everything in each book is explained once you have found the answer to that question.

For example, the book of Proverbs is a book of *proverbs*. Would you believe it – it is not a book of *promises*. A proverb is a proverb and you must not quote it as if it is a book of promises. Yet every time I have heard a preacher quote it he quotes it as if it were a promise. Now a promise can be utterly relied on to be true, but a proverb is not always true. A proverb is usually true but not always. It is a summary of wisdom, and wisdom comes when you know which proverb to apply to which situation. Take one example. There is a verse that says: "Train up a child in the way that he should go, and he will not depart from it." That is not a promise and many parents know it is not because there are children who have been brought up right who have gone wrong. It usually follows, but not always. So when you are reading from the Book of Proverbs, don't pick a verse out as a promise. It will usually apply, but not always; you need wisdom to know when it doesn't.

So the first question of context as far as the book is concerned is: What sort of a book is it? Why was it written? Who was it written for? Then you begin to understand that everything in that book relates to why it was written. That is why I urge people to read the Bible a book at a time. Somebody asked me, "Are you saying preachers should preach books?" And I will say I wish more of them did, because once you have got a book in your mind, you can read it and understand it. What other book would you treat like you treat your Bible? Imagine a detective novel. How do you read it? Well, I think the best way is to start in chapter thirteen and read half of that chapter. Then go back to chapter six and read a paragraph or two of chapter six. Then, for late night reading, read the last page. Would you read a book like that? Yet people read the Bible like that. A little bit here, a little bit there, and they never get the message. We used to read the Bible right through at Millmead in Guildford — it takes eighty-two hours if you do it, but it was the first time people had heard a book read in church. We go to church and we hear twelve verses here and a bit from another chapter there. It is so bitty. God gave us his word in books. Read it as he gave it, a book at a time. Once you have got the book clear, everything in that book will make sense to you; it is all related to it.

Now people have some favourite passages in Hebrews, but until you know why Hebrews was written there will be parts of that book you don't understand at all. It all relates to the purpose of the whole book. So that is a context.

There are four Gospels: two were written for unbelievers, two for believers. Do you know which? Actually Mark and Luke were written for unbelievers, Matthew was written for new believers, and John was written for old believers, very clearly. Yet people give John's Gospel to unbelievers. Frankly, the first stated verses are too deep for me, they are hoping they will read as far as John 3:6 and realise they need to be born again. I think that is why they give it – or John 3:16 perhaps, they might get as far as that. John was written for mature believers to keep them believing. Matthew was written for young believers, and particularly young Jewish believers; it is a very Jewish book. Mark was written about Jesus' deeds. Luke was adding to Mark Jesus' words. But they were all written for different purposes, and therefore the same content means something quite different in the different Gospels.

Two examples: I have quoted the parable of the feast where people declined to come because they bought a field, or married a wife, or some such thing. In Luke's Gospel the emphasis is on getting every seat filled, "My house shall be filled..." but in Matthew the message is for believers who haven't bothered to change—basically the same story. The lost sheep in Luke is a lost unbeliever; the lost sheep in Matthew is a backsliding believer. We must go and look for both. But you see the same story has a different message according to the Gospel it is in. Take the book of Ecclesiastes. It is full of truth, but not necessarily God's truth. That is meant to shock you. There are parts of the Bible that are not God's truth; they are inspired by the Holy Spirit, but they are not part of God's truth. Ecclesiastes tells you the life of a man who was godless, who had a limited tunnel vision of this world under the sun, never got his vision above the sun, and he was totally concerned with this life. He got to the end of life feeling, "What's it all about? I've got nowhere." One of the things he says in that book (it is in your Bible) is, "I've found only one man in a thousand that I could trust, but not one woman." Have you ever had a preacher tell you that? I have taken it, because it is truth. It is not God's truth; it is a man who had seven hundred mothers-in-law. They told me in Sunday school he was the wisest man in the Bible. Can you credit it? He had three hundred mistresses on top of his seven hundred wives, and he said, "I've not found a woman I can respect." Of course he hadn't. You play around with a thousand women and you lose respect – all respect for women – overnight. It is true, but it is not God's truth for you.

Consider the book of Job. Three-quarters of the book of Job you must not take as God's truth. It was the advice the friends of Job gave him, which was based on a false assumption through and through, and God said they were giving wrong comfort. I have heard people quote a verse from one of those Job's comforters as if it was God's truth, and it is not. It is truth because it is what they truly said, but it is a negative truth, it is not God's truth. They were telling Job what they thought was the truth, which wasn't, but God has recorded that in his Word so that we know what advice not to give someone who is suffering.

Context is so important. If you just pick a verse out of the Bible and quote it, you are what a dear old lady said to me: "Bible hopping to prove a point." She was criticising the preaching she was getting in her church, but we may do that. We think the Bible is a box full of proof texts and if we quote a verse that settles it, but you may be quoting quite the wrong verse out of context. The next context question is: "Of which covenant are you quoting?" We talk as if there are only two covenants in the Bible, the Old and the New. The word "testament" is a synonym for covenant. So someone has divided my Bible into old and new covenant, Old and New Testament. I don't know who did it so I can't blame them. I know who did the chapters and verse numbers, but I don't know who put "Old" and "New" Testament in — terribly misleading.

People think today three-quarters of your Bible belong to the old covenant, and the new covenant is a quarter of your Bible at the end. What a terrible mistake! There are at least five covenants in your Bible: the one made with Noah, the one made with Abraham, the one made with Moses, the one made with King David, and the one made with Jesus Christ the Messiah, who shed his own blood as the blood of the new covenant. Now of those five, all five are in the Old Testament and all five are in the New. Of those five, only one is called old and only one is called new. The one thing we must never do (but how many churches do it) is putting people under the old covenant – which is not the Abrahamic one, and it is not the Noahic one, and it is not the Davidic one, it is the Mosaic (Moses) one. We Christians are not under the old covenant (the new has replaced it) but the others continue right through the Bible. The Noahic covenant continues or you wouldn't be around today. The Abrahamic covenant continues, as Hebrews 6 makes quite clear. The Davidic covenant continues, but the Moses one doesn't.

I wonder whether in your church you have been taught to tithe your money—that is old covenant. It is not new covenant, but it is the quickest way for a church to finance its way so it is taught as a Christian duty to tithe—it isn't. It would be your duty as a Jew under the old covenant, but it is not your duty as Christians under the new covenant. You are now under the law of giving, not tithing; giving that is sacrificial, giving that is regular, and giving that is cheerful. That doesn't mean putting a grin on when the collection plate comes around; it means God isn't interested in your money if you don't want to give it. That is new covenant teaching. For many people today, tithing is too much to give — a single mother bringing up children, for example. For many others in a church, tithing is far too small. Yet, we teach tithing as a law of Moses; we are not under Moses, and thank God for that. I am breaking Moses' law when I sit and teach. Moses said you must not wear cloth of mixed material. I might be wearing a Marks & Spencer vest made of a mixture of polypropylene and I don't know what else. I am not bothered that I am breaking the law of Moses. I am not under that law — I am under the law of Christ, which is a good deal stricter, incidentally. Moses just said you didn't have to kill anybody but Jesus' law said you mustn't even call them a fool. Moses said you don't get into bed with other than your wife; Jesus said you don't even think about it. The law of Christ is a good deal harder than the law of Moses, but the law of Moses has 613 laws, most of them prohibitions—"Thou shall not." I couldn't keep them all.

I tell people about a flight I took to Israel sitting opposite three rabbis and I proved to all three that none of them kept the law of Moses. Then one of them said, "What are you, Orthodox or Liberal?"

I said, "No, none of those."

He then guessed, "You're a Christian!"

I said, "Spot on", or something similar.

He said, "I suppose you don't think you need to keep all the laws of Moses."

I said, "I couldn't keep them. You can't, I can't."

Then he said, "I suppose you think that Jesus died to set you free."

"Well, he did – from the Law of Moses, not from his own law. I'm bound by that."

So you see, if you find yourself putting people back under the laws of Moses, you have ignored the context. Now that doesn't mean we can forget about them. We read the laws of Moses to find out what God's heart is, how he thinks, but we don't read it as a law for us. Similarly, Gentile Christians were never put under the Sabbath law; Sunday is not the Sabbath anyway, Saturday is the Sabbath. We are not under that law. We observe Sunday, not as a Sabbath, but as the day Almighty God went back to work and started the new creation, a day to celebrate, a day when more new men and women are made than any other day of the week. It is the eighth day of creation. We are living in the second week of creation. We are in the first day of the second week. Think about it. The first part of the new creation was his own Son's body that came out the grave – not to get old and die, but to be immortal and live forever. That is a whole other subject.

My gospel centres in the resurrection, not in the crucifixion. The trouble is that when the Church split in 1054, the Western Church became the Catholic Church and the Eastern became the Orthodox Church—they diverged a thousand years ago. Since then, Western churches have focused on the Cross as the centre of their faith, Eastern churches focus on the resurrection, and for them their Christian faith focuses on the living Christ. I am with them. The crucifixion was vital, but as Paul says, "If we are justified by his death, how much more will we be saved by his life?" I long to see the Cross replaced by the empty tomb, as the symbol of our faith, but I am afraid we have got stuck in the death. Let us move on to the resurrection and the ascension of Christ, without which none of us could be saved at all.

Finally, the context is not just the paragraph or the section, or the book, or the testament; the context is the whole Bible. We must beware of interpreting a verse that runs contrary to the whole Bible teaching on that issue. This is why we need the whole Bible, this is why we need to read it all, this is why we need to study it all, so that whatever we preach on we have got the whole Bible behind us. I was a great admirer of Dr. Martyn Lloyd-Jones—even just the way he said "God" filled me with awe; he said it slowly, he always said "Gooooood", and just the way he said it made me tremble—but he took sixteen years (once a week) to get through the whole letter to the Romans. But I will tell you how he did it: in every study of every verse he brought the whole Bible in. It was not just that passage; you got the whole Bible every time. We need that, not to spin out our series, but we need the whole Bible behind us; we need to be drenched in the whole of scripture to preach on part of it. That of course means systematically studying it ourselves, so that we know it.

Now I will tell you a secret. The congregation in Chalfont St Peter thought that I knew every bit of the Bible backwards because I preached with such confidence each Sunday. Actually, I only knew one chapter better than they did — that is the real truth. As long as a teacher is one step ahead of those he teaches, he is able to be their teacher. I didn't then know the whole Bible as I know it now. I wish I was starting my ministry again! Right now, with all that I have come to know I would do it so differently. When I look at young pastors who have still got a lot of years ahead I would say: devote yourself to teaching the whole Bible, and you won't go far wrong. Now let me add just one or two qualifications to that. First of all, be thankful that God doesn't wait until you know the whole Bible before you can preach any bit of it. He doesn't wait until we are perfect to use us. If he did, then none of us would be used. I am amazed at the patience of God when he can use someone who only knows a bit of the Bible to share his truth with others. God must have overlooked so much that I taught before I knew better. Once you know better, you can't preach it the old way again.

I will give you two examples. One of the most popular verses to preach is, "Behold I stand at the door and knock—if any man hears my voice I will come in and sup with him and he with me." It is a wonderful verse, which is used as an evangelistic sermon so many times and it has got nothing to do with being converted; it has got nothing to do with inviting Jesus into your life. He is talking to a church that has lost him. A church can do that, and it was a very active and successful church. The church in Laodicea was rich and they had big crowds coming — they did not have Jesus attending the meeting, that was all. That was everything. Jesus is saying to that church: "I am knocking at the door of my own church. If anybody will let me in, I'll come back in." Which means a glorious truth: that one member of a church can get Jesus back in. Isn't that exciting? I know there are some who are lonely members of churches that you are finding it difficult to stay in. Well, one member can get Jesus back in — hold on to the promise. But it is not an evangelistic tool. That is Revelation chapter 3.

The second hint is this: you must not assume that just because God blesses your preaching that you have got it right. Again, if God waited until I got everything right, he would still be waiting to use me in preaching. Thank God he is more patient than that. So don't be put off by what I am teaching you and say, "Oh dear me, until I get it all right he'll never use me." No, he can use the ignorant. Once you have found out the true meaning of a verse you can never use it again in the wrong way, though. I once preached on that verse, "Behold I stand at the door and knock." I said, "Won't you please let him into your life? He is standing outside the door of your heart knocking." Of course it was twisting scripture terribly, and God used it because God doesn't wait until you have got it perfect before he uses you. He has still got much to do with all of us.

Thirdly, you do have a constant duty to find the right meaning to a verse. If you are willing to unlearn as well as learn, and willing to revise your ideas, he will reveal new truth to you. I am still finding the Bible the most exciting book to read because every time there is something new, something I didn't realise, something I never saw before. I know no other book in the world that can do that. But have the courage to preach the true meaning, whatever the cost or consequence.

I made a solemn promise to the Lord years ago that I would preach the truth as I understood it. Not that I am infallible, not that I have got it all right, but when I believed I had found the truth in scripture, I promised Him I would preach it, whatever the cost or consequence. I threw my reputation as a preacher away. I am so glad I did because I want people to trust me as a preacher, not to give them what they want, but to give them what they need – to give them the truth. Even if they never ask for me back again, I will preach the truth. That is why my wife always asks me when I get home, "Was that another double visit?" Do you know what a double visit is? Your first and last rolled into one. There are many times I have to come home and say, "Yes that was a double visit. They'll never have me back again, but at least they know that they once heard the truth that sets us free." They will be responsible whether they have me back or not; they will be responsible for what they did with what they heard. Therein lies your security. If you fear people more than God you will never be a preacher of the truth. You will preach what people want rather than what they need, and the Bible is what they need whether it is comfortable or not.

So I have finished the preparation—and I can move now into delivering the message. This is what people think I am going to share. I am going to share it anyway, but they think that lessons for preachers are going to be about our method not message, yet I have spent the whole time so far on the message. I think someone once asked, "Do you think you have the truth, David?" My reply was, "No, but the truth has me." We don't claim to be infallible. I am not the Pope. I once said to a Roman Catholic priest, "I do admire you Roman Catholics, you only have one infallible speaker in your church. We Protestants have hundreds!" It must be a much safer feeling when there is only one man who can tell the truth, but there we are. We now turn to the method of preaching.

We are still in the pastor's study for a few minutes because I have told you: preach it to yourself first and see how you respond. I have heard of someone who recorded his sermon on a tape recorder and played it to himself before he gave it to the congregation, and he invariably went to sleep. So he could hardly blame his congregation. By the way, if all the people who go to sleep during sermons, in the whole of Great Britain on one Sunday, were laid on the floor end to end head to toe, they would be much more comfortable! That is the truth, but it is not God's truth. I love the preacher somewhere in the American South who was asked his method of preaching. He said, "I thinks myself clear, I prays myself hot, and then I just lets go." I think that is, in a nutshell, a good little summary of preparation.

Now you have prepared it all: you have your illustration, your introduction, your conclusion, you have got the bones of it in your mind, and you have your notes. Turning to the actual preaching, content and communication are the two big subjects before us. So far I have been telling you about getting your content right. Now we think about communicating – how to get it across. Again, the preacher who was my model when I was a young man told me this: "David it's not just getting it off your reel, it's getting it onto his bobbin." I know just what he meant even though he was speaking from a mill background. It is not just getting it off your chest, it is getting it into his or hers. It is communication that is important, and not just content; putting it across from pulpit to pew. That is a long journey and not an easy one.

I want to talk first about the physical aspects of preaching because all preaching is body to body. We can't avoid that. We are communicating with bodies. When somebody says to me, "It is so nice to meet you in the flesh," I will say, "I'm usually in the flesh!" I would much rather people were with me in the flesh. I am not encouraged by people saying, "I'll be with you in spirit on Saturday." I don't like preaching to people who are with me in spirit, I would much prefer them in body. Our bodies are important.

"Are you sitting comfortably?" That was the question of the old mother in a radio programme, and she would then say, "Then I'll begin." If you are not sitting comfortably, I am not comfortable. It is important for hearers to be sitting comfortably. When we opened the Millmead centre in Guildford we had a special pew constructed, of which you could keep adjusting the angle, the height, the back and so on. We had people sitting on it for whole services and keep changing the angles until it was right. We wanted a pew that would hold people upright but not let them lounge. We finally got the design right, and it was patented as the Guildford pew. The firm that made it went out of business so you can't buy it now, but we gave the plans to the church where my wife and I worship, and those seats really hold you nicely, giving you the support where you need it. It is important for you to be sitting comfortably, especially if the preacher is going on and on.

Can you hear what is being said? Now of course we can do wonderful things with loudspeakers and amplification and microphone. We can cure a lot of our troubles. But let me just throw some little light on this. Most music amplified has a totally different need to a voice amplified. A voice amplified needs about one and a half seconds' reverberation – that means the time for a clap to die down; whereas most music needs at least four or five seconds reverberation. The buildings we have are usually one or the other. Even given the amplification systems we install, I often have to speak with a system that is designed for music, and it is very difficult to preach with that. Music needs loudspeakers at the front booming out; the voice needs small speakers all the way around at low volume, so that everybody feels you are just six feet away from them. Most churches now go for music and with all the big speakers at the front, and so many wires, I often feel I am preaching in a telephone exchange. It is designed for music. That is great for the music, hopeless for speaking.

Now with what we know today we can adapt our buildings to both music and speech. I design church buildings as a hobby, and I recommend that they have two amplification systems. Judging by all the equipment churches buy, they can afford it and have one for the voice and one for the music—simple. This was the origin of chanting. When they built the cathedrals they had no idea about acoustics. So they would walk into the empty cathedral, and sing up the scale, "La, la, la, la, la.... Ah, that's the note on which the building is amplifying it and vibrating, so we'll say all the prayers on that note, except at the end." That is how it originated. It was a good idea, and it meant that everybody could hear because they were using the building to amplify the sound. Now, of course, you don't need to do that, but people with microphones that amplify still say their prayers as if they are in a cathedral, except at the end. But it began as a very good thing. It is important for people to hear. Now that I am sure you agreed with already, but the next point will be new to you.

It is just as important for people to see the preacher as to hear him. Most people don't realise this, but all of us lip read.

A third of what I say to an audience goes into the eye rather than ears. Hearers read my expression. If I were to turn and face a wall while I spoke, a third of the message would be lost. Viewers "read" my hands, my face, my lips. A television was set in the main high street in Guildford. On the screen was a man saying continually, "Pop, pop, pop," but out of the loudspeaker came a voice saying, "Dad, dad, dad." They asked people to stand in front of the TV set for one minute, and write down what the man was saying. Nine out of ten wrote "Pop". Isn't that interesting? Nine out of ten were reading his lips, and that is the message they got. Therefore, it is very important for people to see the preacher as well as hear him. The problem when you have a flat floor is that the further back you go the more difficult it is to see.

I did once, however, preach to two hundred dogs in Millmead. The dogs came to hear me and gave me close attention because their owners were all totally blind. Whereas the owners listened to me with their heads on one side, the dogs watched me with real attention. Guess what I preached on? I preached on hell. I said, "It is better to lose your sight and go to heaven than keep your sight and go to hell." I asked them to pray for me because I had my sight. There was a dear old lady in her seventies sitting and listening to me, and she had never seen anything all her life. She had always been bitter and resentful that she had no sight, and for the first time in her life she prayed for me because I was sighted. She was converted, and she went back on the bus to Yorkshire, praising the Lord the whole way and singing hymns. I was so glad I preached on hell, though it was a difficult decision because when I asked the Lord, "What do you preach on to blind people?" He said, "Hell." That is not easy, but it proved to be just the right message. The Lord always knows best. So I preached to the dogs because they looked at me.

5

Conviction

We have been looking at the physical side of the congregation: that they should be comfortable, that they should be able to hear—what is the point of preaching if people can't hear? And that they should be able to see. When I design churches, I design them so that everybody can have a direct view of the preacher without having to look around anyone else's head—that is important. There are one or two other things for the congregation.

What is the ideal shape of a congregation? Have you ever thought about that? The answer is if the congregation is fewer than twenty, three quarters of a circle is the ideal shape. I am thinking of how you place the chairs. Between twenty and two hundred people, the ideal shape is a half circle. Over two hundred, the third shape is a quarter circle. If you have been to the Millmead Centre in Guildford, that was the shape of the congregation, and it needs that narrow shape. Now when you have got chairs you can arrange the congregation to some extent but you are limited by the building.

Now let us talk about the preacher's body, which is very important to preaching. First of all, the voice — which is one of the most delicate musical instruments God has ever made. It is the preacher's vehicle; I couldn't preach to you without my voice, but there are many preachers who don't realise that just as you have to train yourself to use any musical instrument—guitar, piano, whatever—you need to train your voice. The voice is very important, and indeed it is the most important thing about the preacher's body. One very common mistake is to preach from the back of the mouth. When you preach from the back of the mouth it doesn't come out very well. We did have at college someone who came once a term, and had each of us on our own for half an hour, and the first thing he taught me was to talk with the front of my mouth and not talk in the throat. Germans particularly have a very guttural accent in the back of the throat. I don't know if you have noticed, they find it very difficult to preach from the front of the mouth. I have noticed that when the Holy Spirit gets hold of someone he really opens their mouth wide and the voice comes to the front.

Another common mistake preachers make is to let their voice drop at the end of sentences. Have you heard preachers talk like that? At the end of every sentence it fades away as if someone is on the volume control and turns it down.

It is amazing how many spoil their preaching with their voice. Again, if your voice is too high, think of Margaret Thatcher, who in the beginning of her political career had far too high and strident a voice, and it sounded as if she was always complaining. Somebody took her in hand and brought her voice right down and it greatly improved her speaking. Again, if your voice is too high it can get very tiring for people to keep listening to that high voice. When you are complaining about something you tend to put your voice up. So keeping the voice down is another important thing, but the biggest thing is to introduce variety to your voice so that you are not speaking on one note all the time — or your voice will be monotonous and you will go on speaking in that tone of voice all the sermon. By the end of it people are just physically tired of listening to it. Your voice is a wonderful instrument—it can convey so much of your feeling, of your inner thoughts and being. It is a voice that

God wants you to use, but I advise a number of preachers to find a voice production person and let them give a little tuition. If you are going to be preaching for a lifetime then learn how to use your voice; the lyrics are often good but the music is poor.

By your vowels people will know where you come from; by your consonants they will know what you are saying. Again, another favourite error is not to pronounce your consonants, and to miss out the "t"s and the "p"s and just assume that people know what you are talking about. Dialect is all in the vowels. You may have noticed that I have short "a"s. I don't talk about "dahncing" with people, but dancing with them. That is my northern background; you can tell I am a northener by my short "a"s. I come from Newcastle not "Newcahstle". So my "a"s are always short, but I have had to kill my home dialect, not that I ever had much.

So if you have a strong dialect or accent, get some help in overcoming it and God will give you a wider reach. Anything else? Mumbling – it is amazing how many do that. Others shout all the time, but vary your volume and pitch otherwise you can't blame people for going to sleep. Your voice is a wonderful gift of God, but using it properly does not come naturally. You may be musical but you will still have to learn how to play an instrument.

Now what about the preacher's eyes? A very important part of communication is through the eye. I try very hard to look at everybody once during a sermon because I want them to feel I am talking to them. Eye to eye contact is very important. That is why having notes rather than a manuscript is such a help, because if you can preach from notes ninety percent of the time you can look at the people you are trying to communicate with. Otherwise you are tied down and you are reading things. Next to the voice, I think the eyes are the most important part of a preacher. I know preachers who love to see the whites of the eyes of the people in the pew, but you know what I mean by that. Use your eyes as well as your voice as God gave you them to use. I suppose one of my most frequent expressions is asking you something. To do that I raise my eyebrows; I know I have got into the bad habit of doing that constantly and looking at people. Are you getting me? Are you answering me? Are you understanding this? I am trying to cure it; someday I might manage to.

The face is an amazing instrument, isn't it? It has so many separate muscles, and you can make them express almost anything. You can express fear, horror, joy. So don't be afraid to let people see what you are feeling inside. One compliment (I believe it was) was made by a member of our choir who said, "David, I've never known you to preach without tears in your eyes." That moved me. Where to I don't know! But I feel things deeply and I am not ashamed of tears. Why not? They are often tears of joy, funnily enough. But don't be afraid to let your feelings show, and your face as well show. Your face is where the glory of the Lord appears too—the Shekinah. It is such a pity, I think, when we cannot see each other's faces in church, because the glory of the Lord never appears on the back of heads. Have you ever noticed that? So when you are sitting in a pew behind someone else you never see the glory. As the preacher I can see the glory when it comes in your face, but you can't, except in mine. Let the feelings come out. If you are happy, show it; if you are sad, show it. Because I told you earlier, we need to help people *feel* the Word of God. If the preacher can't feel it then the congregation certainly won't.

What about the hands? There was one speaker in Jerusalem, and bless him, I thanked him for his speech which was magnificent—it was one of the best I have ever heard, but I said, "Why, when you were offering us the biggest challenge to our hearts, did you put your hands in your pockets? Your body language was almost contradicting what you were saying." Hands, again, are a wonderful expressive part of our body, but putting them in pockets says, "This is casual; this doesn't really matter." I really felt led to tell this brother, and he took it in good spirit—it was given in good spirit.

I know we are in an age that likes people being casual, but you are dealing with serious issues. He was talking about judgment for Christians, and that was a very serious subject—but his whole physical stance was contradicting it. Now, I have experienced many preachers' hands in the wrong places. One preacher I know has only one gesture to emphasise anything. Then there is another who has very nervous hands, and it is a terrible distraction. If your hands won't work with you, then just keep them by your side. But hands can appeal to people—hands can express so much. Preaching is physical, and we have to recognise that and see that it is using every part of our body.

What about our feet? I never use my feet to walk when preaching. It has become the craze since the American television evangelists started walking around to give an appearance visually of movement and life. But I will never forget listening to a top barrister in London, who said to me: "Watch the counsel for a defence when they are summing up to a jury. If they are sure of their case, if they are sure their defendant is innocent, they keep their feet still. If they are not sure of their case, their feet move around." Well, when I preach I am sure of my case and I want people to know I am sure. Even when I am not sitting, when I am standing, my feet are still, and they stay in the same place – because I have got a case to present that is a hundred percent sure, and I don't want uncertainty to communicate itself. Don't take that as a criticism of your preacher if he wanders around, but I would rather he didn't, because many times it means turning away from part of the congregation. When you turn around, you are turning your face from the other half. When you are wandering up and down, congregations develop "Wimbledon" problems—I just throw that out because it is what I was told. If you are sure of your case, keep your feet still and present your case with the rest of your body. In the days of having a sound microphone stuck in front of you, you had to stand still. Now they have horrible things that hook on your ear. In Taiwan I had to wear something I have to call a harness! I felt as though I was being harnessed up like a horse with equipment that goes around the back of the head and hooks over the ears. I felt most uncomfortable, and there was something stuck there that tickled the whole time. I am happy with a stand microphone because it keeps me still. Let every other part of the body move, but I believe in feet firmly planted on the foundation of truth – and keep them that way.

All that is on the preacher's body, I will just say a little bit about clothes. As an ambassador for Christ I cannot dress in a sloppy manner. I know it is the "in thing" to be casual, and I am not pleading for Sunday clothes, though I do wonder at the fact that people today seem to dress not for the Lord but for themselves. If I were going to Buckingham Palace to meet the Queen, I would not go in jeans. If we are going to meet the King of kings, then I do think we need to dress accordingly. Now that is just my preference and my opinion, I am not presenting it as more than that. I think that is the question: "Who am I dressing for? Myself or the Lord?" Certainly I would not want to preach if I am looking like I am just off for my holidays. I believe the Lord needs to be honoured, and I do that.

All that is the physical side of preaching. Now let me come to a deeper side of communicating mentally – reaching people's minds. I often say that the greatest unexplored territory in the world is between your ears. The most frequent comment I get after preaching is, "Well you certainly gave us something to think about." It is said in a tone of mild reproach, as if I didn't come to church to think, and a slight resentment that I made people think. But I believe we are to love God with all our minds. Preaching is not only body-to-body, but mind-to-mind. Now how are we going to achieve that? We want people to think God's thoughts. We want them to have an understanding of God's words. So how are we going to do that?

The first thing I'm going to mention is language. I made a choice early in my ministry that I would use Anglo Saxon language, rather than Latin language. There are two languages spoken in Britain. One is spoken in the universities, and in many pulpits of those who have been to university, and it is Latin English. Latin, of course, was the language of the Bible for centuries in this country. Even when ordinary folk didn't understand it, it was still in Latin. The Catholic Mass until the twentieth century was all in Latin, whether people understood or not. The two different Englishes that are spoken are Latin English and Anglo Saxon English. The reason why the Authorized King James Version of the Bible remained so popular for so long was that it was in Anglo Saxon English. Most modern versions have been done by Oxbridge scholars and are Latin English.

The *New English Bible* came out, a version which was supposed to be for the ordinary people in the street. When I read it, I found it was Latin English right through. Here is a phrase from it: "Oracular utterance". Do you understand that? Do you think a bus driver understands that? I'll tell you a bus driver is very familiar with oracular utterances when somebody cuts across the front of him, but he doesn't know it as that. One of my professors in Cambridge was Professor C. H. Dodd, who was then considered the top New Testament scholar in the country. He was Chairman of those translating the New English Bible. He got on the train in Cambridge and went to London, to Smithfield Market, where the butchers were, to find what people would say today instead of "the fatted calf". In Luke 15, the story of the prodigal son: "Let's kill the fatted calf." The scholars at Cambridge had thought up six alternative phrases. Dodd got the butchers together and said, "Which of these phrases would you understand most easily?" He read the list. The butchers shook their heads and said, "We wouldn't use any of those. We talk about the fatted calf." He came all the way back to Cambridge having gone all the way and spent a whole morning to find that out. So it did get into the New English Bible.

What is the difference between the two languages? One is a very direct language used by ordinary people in the street; the other is used by scholars, students and professors. Many pulpits in this country are dishing out Latin English the whole time. The difference is between very direct and very picturesque language and very abstract, multi-syllable words. Let me give you illustrations. Sweat, perspiration — one of those is Anglo Saxon, one is Latin. The Authorized version of the Bible was Anglo Saxon. "A city set on a hill cannot be hidden" – simple, short words, picture language, you can see it. "A metropolis on an elevated location cannot be concealed." That is Latin English. Are you beginning to get the feel of it?

The New Testament was written in Greek as I am sure you know, but there were two kinds of Greek. There was Koine Greek, which was the language of the street, and there was Classical Greek, the language of the Greek scholars. The New Testament was written in Koine Greek; it was the language of the street — short words. Winston Churchill was a master of both languages, but when he broadcast to the people of Britain in World War II he used only five thousand

Anglo Saxon words. When he wrote his books he used twenty five thousand Latin words. Let us think of some of the words you hear in church: justification, sanctification, glorification. Those are all Latin English—long abstract words.

I love the New Guinea version of the New Testament, which is in Pidgin English, which is a very simple form of English, nearer to the Anglo Saxon. Instead of "justification" it has, "God, he say I'm alright."

I said, "Lord, help me to preach in Anglo Saxon English." Use simple, picturesque words. When Churchill wanted to raise his army's morale, he didn't say, "I have nothing to offer you but sacrifice, sorrow, labour and perspiration." None of those words would touch your emotion. But he did say, "I have nothing to offer you but blood, tears, toil, and sweat." That phrase has gone down into history, and is still quoted many years later. He said, "Never was so much owed by so many to so few." That too has gone down into history.

Short words, simple Anglo Saxon words. Because the Authorized Version was based upon a previous translation by William Tyndale, who was Anglo Saxon to his fingertips, the Authorized Version has the same simplicity. The only difficulty is that many of the words have changed meaning. In fact, some words have swapped meanings since the Authorized Version. The word "let" in Elizabethan English meant "to prevent", and the word "prevent" means "to allow". So there are two words that have swapped places. We still have in Old English "without let or hindrance", but to us the word "let" means to allow something; to let someone do something. So we cannot use the Authorized Version now, except that there is somebody around called the New King James. I am trying to find out who he is! There is a new King James who has produced the old King James Version updated, and they have had to change words around. Most modern versions have been done by university scholars, who have this preference for Latin English. Try to get a version that has more Anglo Saxon English, but, in preaching, please learn the difference between those two types of English and, I beg you, use Anglo Saxon. Language is one of the first ways of helping people's minds to accept the truth of God's Word.

The second thing is pace. Now I am told that people can't listen for more than ten minutes today, but I think it is a lie. People can listen for a long time provided your pace is good. By pace I don't mean speed, I speak relatively slowly, but give my hearers a very brisk walk through ideas. Somebody did a mathematical analysis of one of my sermons and found seventy different ideas in a fifty-minute sermon. So we were changing mental course seventy times in fifty minutes. It was not that I was speaking quickly, but I was thinking quickly, and we were moving quickly from one thought to another. I have found that is what keeps people's interest – going for a brisk walk mentally, rather than spinning things out intermittently.

Some people can preach for five minutes and it seems like twenty-five; they have a gift of saying the same thing over and over again in different ways. I believe that pace is the way to keep people's interest. They may not remember the seventy ideas, but you have much more chance of people remembering one, because a different idea will touch a different person. They will feel they have heard from God, even if there is only one of those ideas that stayed with them. You are more likely to reach more people than with one idea spelled out for seventy minutes. I just throw that all out because most people don't realise that mental pace is important—moving swiftly from one idea to the next.

Above all, clarity is so important. I have always made my objective a twelve-year-old boy. I want a twelve-year-old boy to know what I have said and to understand. Nothing gives me a greater thrill than when a twelve-year-old boy comes up and says, "That was great!" I know he means it. A twelve-year-old boy is not to be underestimated and I preach a sermon in such a way that he would go home having understood what I have said. The key to that is clarity – you have got to think yourself clearly before you can speak yourself clearly. That is where the preparation comes in. If you have really got the Word of God clearly in your mind, you will present it clearly in such a way that people can grasp it and go with it. A dear little old lady once said to me, "David you broke it up small enough for me to swallow." She meant it. I said, "Thank God. That is our job, to break it up small enough for people to eat it and swallow it." But we are trying to do more than reach people's minds.

I have emphasised throughout that we need to reach people's hearts—their emotions. The emotions are like the pedal in a car – they provide the power source to move. The car may be a beautiful machine and perfectly understood, but without the pedal it is going nowhere. People respond with their emotions. When they *feel* the Word of God they are ready to *do* something about it, not just when they *think*. If preaching is simply a mental activity, transferring thoughts from one brain to another, it is not getting anywhere. It may be interesting, it may be entertaining, but it is not really going places; it is when people's hearts are touched. That is why I have emphasised when you are preparing, if you are getting excited and you are getting touched and you are getting moved, you are much more likely to have the same response from people. It is not manipulation, though it can be; it is not acting, though it can be, but acting will never take the place of genuine emotion. Manipulating people's feelings by sob stories, I think, is dishonest. But if you feel something genuinely, then you are not manipulating others by sharing your emotions with them.

So much of scripture is emotional: there is one translation of the Bible that leaves all the others standing for communicating the feelings of God's word, and it is Kenneth Taylor's *Living Bible*. If you know that, you will know it conveys the feelings of God more than any other translation, and I have the authority of leading scholars on this. A leading Bible scholar in America said: "By far and away the best translation for producing God's feelings in your heart is The Living Bible." That is why, when we read the Bible through in Millmead, we used that version. It was easier for people to read, and much easier for them to respond to. Somehow that man has captured the feelings of God better than any Bible translation that we know; I do recommend it highly to you for that reason.

Ultimately, what you are after when you preach is not the mind or the heart but the *will*. The real task of the effectiveness of preaching is what people do about it. I have told you that the conclusion should tell them what you hope they will do, but even if you don't tell them, it is so encouraging when somebody does something as a result of your preaching. I had the honour and privilege of preaching to both Houses of Parliament in Australia. It didn't turn out quite as I expected because the previous day I was in Melbourne not Canberra, and the pastor who was driving me to the airport went slower and slower. I said, "I'm going to miss the plane to Canberra and I'm speaking to the Parliament tomorrow."

He said, "Oh I'll get you there, I've never missed a plane yet." He went still slower and said, "I just have a lot of questions I want to ask you." Well, he got me to the plane, but he didn't get my luggage there in time. I arrived in Canberra, the capital of Australia, in my travelling clothes without anything even to shave with. I thought, "I'm meeting the Parliament tomorrow, and I have to meet them wearing an old shirt." I felt terrible. What was encouraging was that after I had spoken to the Members of Parliament, a Cabinet minister as we left came and shook my hand and said, "I'm going home to rewrite my income tax return." I went, "Boy, one sinner who has repented. The angels must be rejoicing." What a lovely comment on a sermon. Not, "Thank you for the nice sermon." I don't often get that anyway. Hallelujah! Something happened that was real – he was doing something about it. I don't know what I spoke to them about, I still don't remember, but God spoke to him. That was the important thing. His will was reached, and he was changing something he did because of the result. I am sure the angels were rejoicing over that. It is the will. Sooner or later a preacher is seeking to align his hearer's will with God's will – to do it.

One of the key words in the New Testament, which is often overlooked, is the little word of two letters: "Do". Christianity is doing; faith without works is dead. It cannot save if you don't do anything with your faith. When our three children were little they loved a game we called "faith". They would go to the staircase and climb up about four or five steps. I would stand at the bottom with my hands behind my back. They would say, "Daddy, if we jump will you catch us?" I would say, "I might and I might not." This was their version of a video nasty, I think, because they would stand there and say, "Shall we jump?" One would jump, and I would catch them, and then another would jump and I would catch them. They loved this game they called "faith". It said something very real about faith. You may say you believe your daddy will catch you – until you jump you don't know. That is what James was saying in his lovely letter. In chapter two, faith is doing something about it.

I was in a large city in Germany and I said to the congregation, "How many of you believe in me?" There was a dead silence and about five people put up their hands. I said, "Well, that's not much of a response. Let me reword the appeal. How many of you believe that I exist?" Every hand went up. Well I said, "Let's go back to the initial question. How many of you believe in me?" There was a well-dressed lady in the front row who put her hand up with the other five or six. I thought, "Well she looks as if I can bring her into the dialogue." I said, "You said you believe in me, but I don't know if you do. You have done nothing to show it. Now if you gave me your money to look after I would know you believed in me, but until you do something I don't know if you do." The place froze – no smiles, and I knew I had put my foot in it thoroughly. You do that if you challenge the congregation. Afterwards I said to the pastor, "Why did everybody freeze when I said that to the lady?" He said, "She is the richest woman in this town. Her husband owned all the property in the middle of the town, and he died and left everything to her. She is literally a millionairess. You said to her, 'Let me look after your money, and I'll accept that you believe in me.'" So that time it rather fell flat.

You see, believing that Jesus existed, believing that Jesus died, believing that he rose again is not believing in him. James was saying you need to do something to show the Lord you trust him. It is what you do that will reveal if you believe in him, and that is a very important point. We have been used to being taught that faith is a passive thing. Did you just think in your heart, "No"? Faith is action, says James. It is what Abraham did when he was ready to sacrifice Isaac. It is what Rahab did, the prostitute, when she hid the spies of Israel in Jericho. Faith is trust and obedience in the Lord.

So that is what we are after, the will to do something. Jesus told a very simple short parable once. "A certain man had two sons...." No, it is not the prodigal son, it is the other one. "A certain man had two sons, and he said to them 'Go and work in my vineyard.' One said, 'Yes, father,' but didn't go. The other said, 'No, father,' and then he went. Which of the two did his father's will?" That is the simplest parable Jesus ever told. Have you ever heard that preached? Why don't we teach it? It is so simple, but it touches the very heart of our faith. To say "yes" and not do anything is the very opposite of saying "no" and doing it. Jesus is saying that what the Father is interested in is not what you say, but what you do. The word "do" comes all the way through the New Testament. Faith, in the New Testament, is a doing thing. It is active, not passive. It is not just what you think inside, it is what you do outside with what you think inside.

There is one other thing I must declare: preachers can't convict people of sin, or righteousness, or judgment; it is the work of the Holy Spirit. Therefore, even though you have prepared thoroughly, and you have applied all the things I have told you, without the Holy Spirit you will get nowhere in preaching. Depend on him to do his job with what you have said. From the beginning to end of preaching you are totally dependent on the Holy Spirit to teach you what the passage says, to enable you to say it – above all, to use your word to convict people. Convincing their minds is one thing, convicting them is another.

The biggest thrill is when the Holy Spirit has done his work. A well-known preacher was coming out of his pulpit and a person said to him, "That was a great sermon." He replied quickly, "The Devil just told me that." The Devil loves great preaching if it doesn't lead to anything – if it entertains people, if it interests them.

What the Lord wants to see is *conviction*. Conviction comes when you are totally convinced of those three simple facts: sin, righteousness and judgment. You can't convince people of that, humanly speaking. You can apply all the best artillery in the world, but only the Holy Spirit can take your word and produce those three convictions in your hearers. It is those three convictions that will result in something.

So every preach is a spiritual battle, and the Devil hates preaching; it is the one thing he wants to stop in the church. He is succeeding to a large degree. The rumour goes around, "People won't listen to preaching." It is a lie, but the Devil is the father of lies. People say "Dialogue is what people want—they want to discuss things." I just say, "What is the advantage of pooling your ignorance? We need the truth. The word "preach" in the New Testament means: "to proclaim; to tell people the Good News." We are news announcers. We are not there to debate or discuss, though we should listen to questions and answer them adequately, and give people a reason for the hope that is in us. But preaching is not dialogue, it is monologue, though without the Holy Spirit that is all it will be. So, from the beginning of your preparation your prayer is, "Holy Spirit, teach me the meaning of this passage, this verse, this scripture. Introduce me to it so I can understand it, and then as I help people to understand it with me, will you please do your work and convict them?"

www.ingramcontent.com/pod-product-compliance
Lightning Source LLC
Chambersburg PA
CBHW071022080526
44587CB00015B/2452